Teaching Writing

JO PHENIX

THE NUTS AND BOLTS OF

RUNNING A DAY-TO-DAY

WRITING PROGRAM

Pembroke Publishers Limited

Dedicated to my students at
Cashmere Avenue Public School,
Mississauga, Ontario,
who taught me at least as much as I taught them

©1990 Pembroke Publishers Limited
Pembroke Publishers Limited
538 Hood Road
Markham, Ontario
L3R 3K9

Canadian Cataloguing in Publication Data

Phenix, Jo
    Teaching Writing

ISBN 0-921217-54-4

1. Creative writing (Elementary education).
2. English language - Composition and exercises -
Study and teaching (Elementary). I. Title

LB1576.P44 1990   372. 6' 044   C90-095062-5

Editor: David Kilgour
Design: Falcom Design & Communications Inc.

Printed and bound in Canada
9 8 7 6

Teaching Writing

CONTENTS

INTRODUCTION

The teaching of writing has always been part of any elementary school curriculum. It has taken many forms, from rote learning of grammar rules and spelling lists to free-form, relatively haphazard encouragement of purely personal writing. This book is intended to give teachers a basic system of teaching writing that uses the best of the experience of the past along with new knowledge about writing and about learning.

I begin with some basic organizational strategies – setting up file-folders, organizing equipment, etc. – and gradually progress to more complex matters such as the writing process, evaluation, and reporting. No one system will meet the needs of all children, nor of all teachers, so wherever possible I have suggested alternative ways to organize the classroom program and to stimulate learning.

Our children all learned to talk quite naturally, as they participated in the language they heard around them and received appropriate models, feedback, and encouragement. Very few of our students will grow up to become professional writers. However, writing will play an important part in their lives. This book may help teachers provide for their students the kind of knowledge, experience, end encouragement that will enable them to take their place in the world of literacy as readily and as enthusiastically as they did in the world of talk.

The Writing Teacher

Looking back on my own experience of being "taught" to write, I have a view of my teachers as copy-editors. They saw it as their job to eradicate all errors in my grammar and spelling, and to teach me to understand language by analysing it and naming its component parts.

Now we have a different view of ourselves as teachers of writing. We are more likely to see ourselves as artisans, practitioners who understand the process, helping young apprentices refine their craft. We are giving our students more of a stake in their own writing and learning, having them make more decisions and take more responsibility. We are finding out what they are doing, and helping them do it better.

I have had the luxury now of studying several pieces of student writing in detail over a number of years, talking about them, trying to explain them to myself and to others. The more I do this, the more I understand the writers, the writing, and what needed to be done to help. When I was teaching these students, I did not have the time for this study and reflection. Usually the student was there for a few minutes, then the opportunity was lost. If we see our job as one of coaching on the sidelines of the writing, then being a writing teacher means constantly making spur-of-the-moment decisions. I need to have the insights and the understandings at the time I can help the student, not when the moment has passed.

Most of our teaching techniques we have learned through on-the-job training; probably that's the only way they can be learned. It is only by reading more and more pieces of student writing, and talking to more and more students about that writing, that we can develop effective ways to listen to them, to talk to them, and to help them become better writers. We learn in the same way our students do—by trying out new ideas and techniques, seeing how effective they are, reflecting on the feedback we get, and modifying as we go along. Our first job is to create situations in which writing is a natural part of the daily activities of the classroom. Once students are writing freely and purposefully, we can help them refine and extend their range of topics, modes, and skills.

There are no rules about how writing should be done, no rules about how it should be taught. Writing is as individual as the students we teach. Fortunately there is a certain logic in how most writing is done, and certain patterns in the ways most writers work. If we have a good understanding of how writing is done, why it is done, and what it is for, we can better help our students learn to think and act as writers.

The Writing Process

Writing involves having something to say, someone to say it to, language to express it, and a knowledge of standard ways of getting language down on paper. Writing is a process of selecting, organizing, and developing ideas; expressing them in effective language; arranging them in logical sequences; and presenting them in neat, standard forms of handwriting and spelling. Learning to write involves developing increasing skill in all these stages of the writing process.

Writing takes time. It does not normally emerge fully formed in a first draft. For some writers, a first draft is no more than a stream of consciousness, with little form or sequence; for others, it may take the form of connected sentences, with a more logical progression of ideas. Sometimes a first draft may simply be a list of things to be included in the final text, or words and phrases that might be used. To try and produce a finished piece of writing in one sitting is counterproductive. The writing is likely to be more effective if each stage receives the concentrated focus of the writer. For this reason, writing must be seen as a process of shaping, each draft moving closer to the intended result.

Before beginning to write, the writer must establish a purpose for the writing; choose a topic; identify the audience. Plans may then be made for such things as collecting information; selecting the mode of writing to be used; deciding on a format. The writer needs at this stage to form some idea of what the task demands, and how to set about it. For some kinds of writing, it may be useful to allow for an incubation period, during which to think about the topic, talk about it, or perhaps make a few notes, in order to define and redefine the task and begin to sort out ideas. Young children, for instance, often develop ideas through art or play before formulating language to express them in writing.

When the writer is ready to translate the inner speech of meaning into the external speech of language, the first draft may take many forms. Some writers start to write quickly, with little preliminary thought and planning. For them, a first draft may be a way of thinking on paper, in fragmentary language. Others mull over the topic and do more mental organizing during the incubation period, so that when the writing begins, it flows more smoothly and logically. For all writers, this first draft is the time to focus primarily on the content.

During the writing of the first draft, a writer typically makes minor revisions at the sentence and word level, as thoughts are refined while they are in the process of being written. Writers may be observed making false starts, crossing out, and beginning again. Often a writer will pause to reread what has just been written, consider how to proceed, then continue to write.

When the first draft is complete, the writer may make more extensive revisions. These may involve additions to content, deletion of irrelevant material, reordering of information, rewording of sentences, selection of more effective words. The writer may at this stage seek out someone to act as a preliminary audience, to help identify where revision is desirable.

During this process of revision, the writer must view the writing in the role of a critical reader, assessing whether or not the subject has been covered sufficiently and presented clearly. At this point, the writer may also reassess some of the thoughts and opinions presented, as it is quite common for them not to be fully formed before they are written down.

Revision, then, is more than correcting and improving the writing. It is another opportunity for the writer to review ideas and opinions before releasing them to an outside audience. While writing must meet the needs of the reader, it must also satisfy the writer.

When the content is complete, organized, and expressed in appropriate language, the writer is ready to make final decisions about presentation, and to proofread for spelling and punctuation errors. When these are corrected, the writing can be recopied into its final form. The writing is then finished, and the writer must accept responsibility for the creation.

What happens to the writing after the final draft is complete will depend on the writer's original purpose. It may be a letter to be mailed, a poster to be displayed, a report to be shared, a story to be read aloud or published, a piece to be kept private by the author. Without an appropriate disposition, there is no purpose for writing.

If we are going to teach our students to write, we must have them follow the same processes that proficient writers use.

━━ 1 ━━
GETTING STARTED

Setting up Writing Folders

You are likely to get better results if your students write on individual sheets of paper rather than in notebooks. Books are alright for things like journals, which are essentially first-draft writing only, but if you want students to reshape and polish their writing at all, using paper rather than notebooks allows them more flexibility. It is much easier to cut and paste paragraphs, rearrange pages, and insert new material if you are using loose paper. One can often get a different view of one's writing, what fits and what doesn't, if one can set the pages side by side. Also, students are often reluctant to make a mess in a book, which seems more like a permanent record than loose paper. With paper, you get a fresh start every time, and only the final draft needs to be seen by the "public".

This means that students will have to organize a lot of paper. They will often have several writing pieces in progress, as well as finished pieces. Some commercial folders have different spaces for writing at different stages. You or your students might like to design and construct your own folders, with sections that meet your own needs. You might have sections for some of the following:

- "Ideas"
- "Jottings"
- "First-Draft Writing"
- "Work in Revision"
- "Pieces on the Back Burner"
- "Finished Writing"
- "My Best Pieces"

By dividing writing up into sections in this way, you can

help students see that writing is a process in which different things are done at different times or for different purposes.

If you don't feel the need for this kind of organization, manila file-folders are quite adequate to store writing, as long as students take a little trouble to paperclip their pieces and keep them separate.

Using the Folder for Record-Keeping

The writing folder can be a convenient place to keep notes and records. It allows both you and students to record such things as:

- "Stories I have written/published"
- "Future topics"
- "Editing skills I can use"

Storage

You can store folders alphabetically in a file drawer or in a banker's box standing on a desk-top or on the floor. You will need to have a hanging file for each student, so that folders will not fall over. Wherever you store them, it is important that students have access to their folders whenever they need them.

Troubleshooting

With very young children, teach them to remove only their own folders, not the hanging files; otherwise they will never get them back in the right place.

Setting up a Writing Centre

A writing centre may be a place where students actually go to do their writing, or it may be a place where materials and equipment for writing are stored. In either case, having everything students need in one place will cut down on traffic, as well as helping to make them independent. You don't want to be bothered every time someone needs a paperclip.

You will need to provide such things as:

- pens, pencils, crayons, markers, etc.
- different kinds of paper—plain, lined, half-and-half, different sizes

- stapler, scissors, three-hole punch, staple remover, paperclips
- dictionaries, wordbanks, etc.
- storage for writing folders

As the year goes on, you might also collect things like:

- theme-word lists
- student-made glossaries/dictionaries
- cheat-sheets (reference lists of hard-to-spell but often needed words, such as days, months, names)

Make "outline mats" for the storage shelf to help keep things tidy. Trace around each object to show where it is to go. At the end of the day or period, you will easily be able to see if anything is missing.

If this is a writing work centre, the students will need to know when they are to go there, how long they should stay, what they should do while they are there, and what to do when they are finished. If you want to establish a minimum time for writing, provide an oven-timer for those who cannot yet tell the time.

If you are not careful, all the pencils or pens will be gone by the third day of school. To avoid this, store them in cans with only four pencils to a can; then they can easily be checked regularly. I had a student check the cans four times a day, always before the children left the room for recess or to go home. It's amazing how quickly they find the pencils when they are waiting to leave.

Troubleshooting

If you provide erasers, students may spend more time rubbing words out than writing them in. Teach them to cross out! Supply erasers for use only at final draft stage, where neatness is important. In this way you can save students a lot of time, and teach them something about the writing process. It is important for them to know when neatness matters and when it doesn't. It is as much of a problem if they think it *always* matters as if they think it *never* matters.

16

You can create a "Final Draft Kit", to be used only for final drafts and books for publishing. Use a box, and put in it items like these:

- erasers
- better-quality paper, letterhead paper
- calligraphy pens and markers
- special markers for illustrating
- 11" x 14" paper to fold for book pages
- construction paper cut to size for covers
- ready-made covers
- needles and thread for sewing books together
- book-binding tape for spines

Make sure the students know that none of this is to be used until thorough editing has been done and everything is as perfect as it can be.

Getting Students Started on Daily Personal Writing

Once you get organized, the routines of personal writing time should operate without constant monitoring. Then you will be free to be a writing teacher. You can't have writing conferences unless the room runs itself without you.

Students need to know these things about their personal writing time:

- They will be expected to write every day.
- They will be choosing their own topics.
- They will be talking to you and to each other regularly about their writing.
- They must know how to get out and put away their writing folders.
- They must know where to find and how to use materials.
- You are not the only person in the room they can go to for help and advice. They are quite capable of helping each other.

There are several possible ways of organizing writing time:

The Writing Period

You may have a period during which all the students are writing at the same time.

Advantages:
- You can establish when students are to start and stop writing.
- You can control the length of time students spend writing.
- Everyone can contribute to an atmosphere of busy writing.
- You know when the students are available for conferences.

Disadvantages:
- The time is not flexible. All the students must stop writing at the same time, no matter how engrossed they are.
- You have fewer options and less time for arranging conferences.
- The students may feel they have less control over writing conditions.

Writing Groups

You may have different groups work at a writing centre at specified times during the day. Here are some tips on this arrangement:
- Set up a timetable so that students know which group they are in, and when it is their time to write.
- You will need a way to indicate when the time is up. Using an oven-timer is better than having students watch the clock.
- For students who cannot yet tell the time, you could use a timetable like this:

List of names	Writing time
Kate	First job
Madhu	
etc.	

Lois
Vinay
etc.

Advantages:
- You can control the minimum time everyone spends writing.
- Students have the option of staying longer than the minimum time if they wish or need to.
- You have more possible times in which to hold writing conferences.

Individual Writing Time

You may leave it up to the students when and for how long they write.

Advantages:
- Students can spend as long as they need writing.
- Students have to take more responsibility for themselves.
- They may feel they have more control over their writing.

Disadvantages:
- Young children have little concept of time; they may spend two minutes or two hours on writing. You will need to have some way of making sure they spend enough time writing.
- It is hard to organize a systematic way of having conferences if you do not know when any particular student will be writing.
- It is more difficult to encourage students to work together.
- Observation of the students while they are writing is more difficult.
- You and other students may not be available when help is needed.

Whichever way you choose, encourage a workshop atmosphere for writing. While the students are writing, move around the group, help them get started, or answer questions.

19

Encourage them to work together and help each other. There will be some buzz of conversation, but it will be a busy, generally productive noise; the students will need to learn at what level their talk becomes disruptive. When the students have settled down to writing, you can call individuals or groups for conferences.

Training and Using Volunteers

Adult volunteers or older students can help in the day-to-day running of the writing program:

- They can be an audience for the students' writing.0
- They can sit in on group conferences while the students comment on and question each other about their writing.
- They can take dictation from those who are just learning to spell.
- They can help with proofreading and editing.
- They can provide standard spellings for personal word banks.
- They can type or print pieces for publication or display.
- They can help make book covers and bind completed books.
- They can make sure writing supplies are replenished when necessary.

Using volunteers will allow you to spend more time helping the students in their composing and revising, where the real teaching about writing goes on.

Any volunteers you use in your classroom will need to know something about teaching writing. You want them to support what you are trying to teach, not work against it. Here are a few simple rules you can give them to start with:

- First-draft writing is for ideas only. Never talk about spelling, neatness, or handwriting at this stage.
- If students ask how to spell words during first-draft writing, tell them to do the best they can, and you will help them edit when they are finished.
- When students share their writing with you, respond to

what the writing is about as an interested listener, just as you would if the students were talking to you.

- Do not correct a student's work unless the student asks for editing help.

As your volunteers become more used to the way you and your students work, you can allow them a little more flexibility. If you want to keep your volunteers interested, make sure they are spending most of their time working with the students rather than carrying out housekeeping tasks.

2
CONFERENCES

Making Time for Conferences

As a general rule, the more often you talk to a student about writing in progress, the more helpful you can be, and the more teaching opportunities you will have. In the ideal situation, you might talk to each student before the writing is started, after the first draft is written, during subsequent revisions, and again during the editing stage. With the number of students most teachers have to deal with, this is very rarely possible. What you need to do is to work out a system so that you can confer with the students regularly. Then, once in a while, make an effort to follow one piece of writing through all its various stages so the student can see how the drafting process works as a whole.

You must see the students as often as possible. If you don't, they will come to you with pages and pages of writing, and it may be too late to do anything with it. You will find it hard to choose a focus for your teaching, and students who are not used to or skilled in revision may see the job as too overwhelming.

You may decide that for a start you will meet with eight students a day. If you can meet with ten students a day, you can see each one in a class of thirty every three days or so. If you can't talk to ten students in an hour-long period, you are probably spending too much time on your conferences. Aim to work up to half your class or fifteen students, whichever is greater, every day.

If you have trouble finding time for so many conferences, remember:

- You don't always have to read the piece of writing. Get

the writer to tell you about it. This teaches the student to step outside the writing and see it from a reader's point of view.

- Some students will need only a word of encouragement, and maybe a brief pointer or question from you, to be able to get back on track and continue writing.
- You are not the only person in the room who can give help and advice.
  (See "Peer Conferences" in this chapter, and "Training and Using Volunteers" in Chapter 1.)
- Conferences do not all have to be held during writing time. You can talk to a student about writing at any time when others are working independently.
- Time spent on conferences is time well spent; sacrifice something else for them.

The conference is your most valuable teaching time, and the student's prime learning opportunity. You will never have enough time; just do the best you can.

Remember: it is better to do something useful once a week than to do something useless every day.

Troubleshooting

If the students seem to be doing a lot of writing which you never see or talk to them about, don't worry. Regard this as their practice time. If you can read everything they write, they are not writing enough.

Here are some alternative ways in which you could organize your conference time:

Regular Conference Time
Set up a schedule so the students know when it is their turn to meet with you. Put up a list of names for each day of the week, and work your way through it systematically. This is a relatively random approach, since you will not know at what stage each student's writing will be. You will not always be available when the students particularly need you. However, if you are seeing each child every two or three days, you should catch them at all the different stages within a short time, and you may frequently

see one piece of writing on more than one occasion before it is finished. This approach ensures that you give all the students equal time.

Sign-up

Students may sign up during the day or a writing period to indicate that they would like a conference. (This is more suitable for older students – the little ones always want you every day.)

Use a pad made of newsprint strips stapled together. When you are ready, tear off the top strip and call up the students who have written their names on it in turn. Older and more experienced students may sign their names and their reasons for wanting a conference. This is good training for them, as they will come prepared with whatever they want to discuss or ask about.

You may want to give some guidelines about when a conference might be appropriate. For example: if you have a problem with your writing; when you have finished a first draft; before starting a final draft; whenever you need help.

If you use this system, you will have to keep a record of students you see and when. Some students will never sign up. Some will go for long periods before signing up. You will need to find another system to ensure these do not get missed. You do not want them to go on working on their own too long before you are involved.

As You See a Need

As you observe the students at work, you will sometimes see one who seems to need help. If you start your writing time by moving around the group and having a brief word with each student, you will naturally spend longer with those who need help than with those who don't. One problem with this is that students who just keep writing tend to get less of your time than those who can't get going. Quantity isn't everything. You will need to keep a check on which students you spend time with each day, so some do not get overlooked for long periods.

A Combination of the Above

You might divide your time into:

- regularly scheduled conferences
  (with a timetable posted)
- additional conferences called at a student's request
  (using a sign-up sheet)
- additional conferences called as you see a need
  (prompted by your observations of the students and their
  writing)

This is the best way to meet everyone's needs, including your own, but is more difficult to organize. You could save fifteen minutes of your conference time each day for specially requested meetings. Or you might stick to a regular schedule during writing time, and call students for additional conferences at other times of the day.

Troubleshooting

Avoid line-ups at your desk. Students should spend their time writing, not waiting. And it is hard to concentrate on one student when another is breathing down your neck. Make disturbing a conference one of the cardinal sins of the classroom.

If students feel they are stuck or finished and cannot do anything without seeing you, you must provide them with alternatives:

- "Try and solve your own problem."
- "Find someone else to help you."
- "Browse through your writing folder and find something else you could work on or reread."
- "Skip over the hard part and go on with another part of the writing."
- "Start a new piece of writing."
- "Sign up for help later."
- "Use your own good judgment about what you should do."

Setting the Mood

The Comfortable Conference

In his observations of talk between a mother and her child, educational psychologist Jerome Bruner noticed an interaction which was particularly effective in helping the child achieve an intended outcome. He called this kind of interaction "scaffolding". An intended outcome might be to build a tower of blocks, to learn how something works, or to write a postcard to a friend. In effective scaffolding, the adult responds to what the child has initiated, and helps the child develop concepts and language necessary for the task. Simply put, it means finding out what children are trying to do, and helping them do it better.

When the intended outcome is a piece of writing in the classroom, you can provide scaffolding during a conference. Here are some things you can do:

- Let the student know you are interested in what he or she is writing.
- Make the setting as predictable as possible; avoid surprises.
- Establish a routine to determine when a conference will take place (e.g., at the student's request, at a certain time during the week or day, etc.).
- Make the setting as comfortable as possible.
- Have a special place for talking about writing. Make it as attractive and as private as possible.
- As a collaborator, sit beside the writer rather than across a table.
- Find out what it is the writer is trying to do.
- Talk with the writer about the topic to develop language about it.
- Reverse roles; encourage the student to explain what he or she knows about the topic, and to initiate questions and discussion.
- Make sure that the student plays the principal role; follow, don't lead.
- Make the writer aware of alternatives in language and organization.

- Encourage the student to ask questions and express opinions.
- Give the writer time to try new approaches and to experiment.
- Leave decisions up to the student.
- Do not be judgmental – be helpful.

Effective scaffolding can help the student clarify intentions, experiment with language and form, and retain control of the writing while still allowing you to give advice and teach new concepts and skills. Writing conferences are more productive when both you and the student feel at ease. Then you can both concentrate on the piece of writing in a constructive atmosphere.

The Structure of a Conference

Both you and your students will feel more comfortable if you know what is going to happen in a conference. If the students know what to expect, they will be more ready to trust you and talk to you about their writing.

It might help you to organize your talk with the students if you think of each conference in three parts:

- Beginning – getting the student talking
- Middle   – the "meat" of the conference
- End   – sending the student back to work

Each part has a different focus:

Beginning

Get the student talking about the writing. It often helps to ask a question. For example:

- "What are you planning to write about?"
- "How is your writing going?"
- "Did you manage to solve that problem we talked about last time?"
- "Which piece would you like to talk about today?"

Or you could start by repeating what the writer already knows:

- "You say here that volcanoes are caused by ..."

Then—wait! If the student does not seem about to talk to you, look expectant, and wait. You don't want the conference to be a question-and-answer session. When the writer comes to you already knowing what to talk about, you know you are doing well.

Middle

There are more options in this part of the conference, because it is here that you will choose what you will focus on and help the student with. What you choose will depend on the stage of the writing and the experience of the writer. It is probably a good idea to stick to one section, and to choose only one or two subjects for discussion:

1. Content (before and during early-draft writing)
  Topic
  - Help the student select a topic, if necessary.
  - Encourage the student to talk about the topic.
  - Show an interest in what the student is writing about.
  - Help the student clarify intentions. (Discuss purpose and possible audience.)

  Focusing
  - Help the student to narrow down the topic. Rather than "Japan", for example, select "Sumo Wrestling", or "How Pearl Divers Work".
  - Find out what the writer is really interested in.
  - Help the writer stay on topic. Draw attention to irrelevant material. ("I'm not sure what this part has to do with your main topic.")

  Expanding
  - Help the writer to recall information or generate ideas. ("Where else did you go on your trip?" "What other disasters might your characters experience?")
  - Ask questions. ("What did you do when it started to rain?" "Do you really think people would behave that way?")
  - Share your own experience. ("Did I ever tell you about the time I ...")
  - Suggest resources. ("Maria knows a lot about stamps. Have you talked to her?")

2. Process (after first draft)

- Help with revision.
- Focus the writer on the process of writing. ("What do think you should do next?")
- Discuss possible ways to organize the writing.
- Teach revision shortcuts, such as arrows indicating where material is to be moved, omission marks, cut-and-paste.

3. Evaluation (after some revision has been done)

- Review purpose and audience.
- Help decide whether the writing is finished, needs more revision, needs more research.
- Together, decide whether the piece is to be shared, displayed, published, etc.
- Encourage the writer to reflect on the writing. ("What made it difficult?" "How does it compare with other pieces I have written?")

4. Editing (before writing a final draft)

- Give instruction on a particular skill.
- Help the writer identify and correct spelling errors.
- Help the writer check punctuation and other print conventions.
- Help the writer prepare pieces for publication/display.

End

Make sure that the student knows what to do next. This will depend on what you have talked about during the middle part of the conference:

- Continue with the writing.
- Add more details to the writing.
- Reorganize information.
- Start a new piece.
- Do some more research.

During the course of the writing, the writer will generally be following the above sequence from top to bottom, with some repetition of sections. Most of the time, you will jump into the middle of this process. The stage of the writing will tell you what kind of intervention is appropriate. When you look at a piece of writing, you will need to first identify which part the student is working on; then you can choose your focus for the conference.

Keeping It Brief

We often fall into the trap of trying to do too much with a piece of writing. Then our conferences get too long, and we don't see students often enough. If we spend too much time students will forget most of what we discuss with them before they get back to the writing. In most cases, "little and often" is more productive than letting days go by without talking to a student at all. To start with, aim for an average of four minutes for each conference. Students who need a little more than this will be canceled out by those who need less.

As a general rule, if you choose one thing to focus on, that is enough. The skill lies in choosing the one thing that will most help the student at that time. What follows is a guideline you could start out with.

During First-Draft Writing and Early Revisions

Work on the content. Your aim is to have the writer analyse what is there and see where it could be improved. Ask yourself these questions as you read the writing or talk to the student; then choose one to focus on with the student:

- Is there enough information/detail?
- Does the text leave the reader with unanswered questions?
- Is it accurate?
- Is it interesting?
- Is it to the point?
- What would make it better?

When Content Is Complete

Work on organization. Your aim is to have the writer look at how the information/ideas are presented. Ask yourself these questions; then choose one to focus on with the student:

- Is it in a logical order?
- Are the beginning, middle, and ending alright?
- Should it have headings?
- Are there parts that would be better as lists, graphs, etc.?
- Does it need paragraphing?
- What would make it clearer?

When It Is Organized

Work on editing. Your aim is to help the student learn to proofread for errors, and to know how to go about correcting them. Choose which of these to focus on with the student:

- Are there spelling errors you will have the student correct?
- Is there a spelling concept you can teach through a word in the piece?
- Is there a punctuation mark you can teach the student about?
- Should the student do a final draft? (Is there to be an outside audience?)
- How could the writing be presented?
- What would make it look better?

When you get to know your students well, you will know which of them are able to focus on more than one point after a conference. Do not rush this. If the students learn one new thing about writing each time they come to you, they are doing well.

Remember, if there is still a lot wrong with a piece of writing, there is always next time. It is better to teach one thing well than to try for too much and teach nothing.

Peer Conferences

Having students share their writing with one another can give them more opportunities to talk about and reflect on their writing. As they read their pieces aloud or talk about what they are trying to do, they may come to look more critically and analytically not only at one another's writing, but at their own. They can often be as helpful as we can in helping each other to choose topics, asking questions for clarification, pointing out which parts of the writing they did not understand, adding interesting bits of information, and laughing at humorous parts. And they are often more honest than we are when the writing is dull!

The students can learn to help each other by following the same procedures you use in conferences:

- showing an interest in what the writer is saying
- being positive and supportive
- asking questions where clarification is needed
- offering more information about the topic
- suggesting solutions to problems
- helping with proofreading and editing

Here are a few ways you can get students talking to each other about their writing.

Talking with a Partner

Set aside five minutes at the beginning and/or end of a writing session for students to work with partners. They might tell each other about the writing done or proposed for the day, choose a part to read aloud, discuss a problem, or ask for help. In this way, every student would talk to someone every day about writing.

Group Conferences

Have the students work in groups of four, for about ten minutes. They might take turns to talk about their writing, discuss a problem they are having, ask for help, or choose part of their work to read aloud. You might want to sit in with the groups for a while at the beginning, until they learn what it is they are expected to do. While leaving most of the talking to the group, you can model the kinds of comments and questions that might be helpful to each writer. Alternatively, you could give them a few guidelines to get them started:

- "Tell the writer what you like about the piece."
- "Ask a question about something you didn't understand."

When they become more used to group conferences, you

can extend the experience by having them do some thinking and planning beforehand. Tell them to come to the conference prepared to do one of the following:

- "Tell the group what you are working on, what it is for, and why you chose it."
- "Ask the group's help with something you are having difficulty with."

These kinds of tasks will encourage students to reflect on writing in progress, and assess their own progress in that writing.

When they become used to this kind of talk, they will no longer need your guidelines. As soon as they can decide for themselves what they want to talk about, let them do it.

Learning from the Conference

From time to time, after a group conference, students should take a few minutes to reflect on the group process. You could start this reflection by asking them to discuss one or two specific questions. For example:

- "Was anyone in the group helped today? How?"
- "What problems did your group solve today?"
- "What kinds of things helped your group?"
- "Did anything make your group discussion more difficult?"
- "How did each person in the group contribute?"
- "What might you do differently next time to make your group discussion more productive?"

Group conferences can help your students to learn about writing and writers, as well as about group dynamics:

- They will learn that all writers struggle with blocks, problems, and failures. Their problems are not unique.
- They will learn that talking about one's writing can help one do it better. They are not alone.
- They will learn that it doesn't matter what one starts out with as a first draft; there is usually a way to shape it to what one wants it to be.
- They will learn something about how to help each other.

As they gain experience with peer conferences, they may become more aware of questions they can ask themselves about their own writing. When they can reflect by themselves on their own writing, then they are becoming writers.

3
THE WRITING PROCESS

What Makes a Good Writer

When I was in school, writing was a one-shot deal. The only time we ever got a second try was if the first one was so bad we got a "D". This meant "detention"; we had to stay after school and do the work again. Although the errors were usually all marked, and the teacher sometimes made comments on the bottom of our texts, we were given no help in making the second draft any better than the first: we were on our own again. It was usually a matter of correcting all the "careless" mistakes.

Doing a second draft was a punishment, a disgrace, a sign that one had failed. It was something to be avoided at all costs! What this taught me was that a good writer is someone who can get everything perfect in one try.

This, of course, is not the truth. A good writer is one who works and works to improve the writing, and is not satisfied until it is the best it can possibly be. The number of drafts, the length of time taken, the amount of help and advice given, are irrelevant; it is the quality of the *final* draft, not the first, that counts. It is important for us, as teachers of writing, to understand the processes involved, but it is even more important for the students themselves to understand. If they do not know how to go about the task, they can never be successful.

An understanding of the writing process is important to us for another reason. Because each stage has a different focus for the writer, we can choose just the right moment to teach students the skills and techniques they need. And because they are focusing on the stages of writing *one at a time*, they are more likely to be successful in learning these skills.

Helping Students to Choose Topics

If students claim they don't know what to write about, especially at the beginning, don't be too eager to help. They can become dependent on you, and unable or unwilling to think for themselves. They may be concerned about what it is you want, and worried about doing the wrong thing, rather than thinking about what they have to say. Be prepared to wait them out, even if it means they sit and do nothing for a few days. They will not learn by having someone else do their thinking for them.

Having accepted this, there will be times when you need to give some assistance. Everyone runs out of ideas at some time, and once in a while it doesn't hurt to jog the thinking a little. Sometimes young children will limit their writing to words they know how to spell, and write a slightly different combination of the same words every day. Sometimes a student may write for a long time on the same topic. This can provide a sense of security and confidence as the writer works with familiar ideas and vocabulary. It can also lead to boring, repetitive writing, and a writer who is afraid to take a risk with something new; this student may need to be nudged into widening the scope. Some students simply do not believe they can write about anything they want, and are waiting for you to tell them what *you* want.

When helping a student to choose a topic, suggest alternative avenues of thinking, rather than providing an idea. When the student does make a choice, there should be real personal commitment to the topic.

Commitment to the topic will come only if the writer has a purpose for the writing. There are two questions a writer should always ask when embarking on a new piece:

- What is it for?
- Who is it for?

There can be a wide variety of answers to these questions:

- There is a letter I need to write.
- I have to record some information so I don't forget it.

- I want to think out an idea.
- I want to write a story to share with an audience.
- I have a bit of language in my head which I like the sound of.
- I want to try out a new technique I have learned.
- I want to fill in my diary.

Often the actual outcome and disposition of the writing will change before it is finished. This may be because the writer's intentions change, because the writing itself changes, or because the original plan did not work. Such changes do not matter. What matters is that the writer has something to work towards while planning and carrying out the writing.

We must try to have our students see their writing as a real-world task rather than as a school subject. Therefore, before asking a student to do any writing in the classroom, we must always ask ourselves this question:

- What's in it for the writer?

Delayed gratification is not a great motivator for children. (It isn't all that motivating for me, either.) This is why the art of teaching is always to create a need in the student for what it is we think they ought to learn. The best way to ensure that our students always have something to write about is to create situations in which writing plays a necessary part.

Here are some ways you can help students to choose topics:
- At the beginning of the writing session, have the students work in pairs for five minutes to tell each other about their writing plans. If one does not have an idea, he or she may be sparked by an idea from the other.
- Have the children share their writing with one another; ideas are sometimes triggered by listening to other pieces and finding out what one's friends and classmates are writing about.
- If you know about any special interest a student has, such as bird-watching or hockey, get the student to talk about it.
- With the student, go back through the writing folder to select the best two or three pieces in it. Discuss how and why the topics of these pieces were chosen.

- With the student, select a piece from the writing folder to be revised or expanded. Then discuss possible additions and changes.
- Get the students to keep an ongoing list of possible topics for future use. This could be done right on their writing folders, and added to at any time the students think of an idea.

Be sure you remind the students that all writers have dry periods and blocks. This is normal. There is nothing wrong with writing nothing for a day or two – as long as it doesn't become a habit.

The Incubation Period

A writer will often begin a piece of writing with no clear idea of how it will develop—the ideas and language are formed as the writer goes along. These ideas may need time to incubate, and the writer may wish to continue the piece over the course of several days, or even longer. Sometimes a writer will leave a piece entirely for a while to work on other ideas. When a writer gets a block and doesn't know how to continue, often the best thing to do is to forget about the piece for a few days, or weeks. Sometimes the piece is abandoned, sometimes it is revisited at a later date. This is normal in the world of writing. It will be normal for your students too.

Looking back over writing periods in my classrooms, I realize that I have often treated writing like instant pudding. I have put my all into motivating the students, then told them to start writing. I have been very upset and anxious when some of them did not seem able to start immediately and keep writing until the job was done. But writing doesn't necessarily work this way.

Incubation sometimes means thinking, which can look a lot like daydreaming or wasting time, and this can make us anxious: we do not know what the students are thinking about, and we are afraid they are doing nothing productive. This may in fact be the case. Nevertheless, we must give thinking its rightful place in the writing process. Let's not deny our students time to think in peace.

Talk can play an important role in this incubation time. Talk, because it is not done alone, is often easier to sustain than thinking or writing, which are essentially monologues. With talk, there are also other people's ideas and insights to add to or contrast with one's own.

Incubation can also mean forgetting a piece entirely for a while. It often seems that ideas sort themselves out in one's head while one is thinking about something else. This means that students may have two or three unfinished pieces of writing in their folders at any one time. This should not be discouraged. Much of the writing the students do will never go beyond the first-draft stage. Writing may legitimately be abandoned at any time the writer does not feel it is worth continuing. The decision about whether to revise or continue should always be that of the students. They may even go back and forth from one piece to another. What matters is that they work on something that interests them, and that they can make progress with.

As the year progresses, the students should be encouraged to reread their old unfinished or unrevised pieces. Their increasing skill in composing and transcribing, or just a period of incubation, may lead them to go back to a piece written many weeks before and finish it or polish it up for publication. On the other hand, they should have the right to abandon any piece they are no longer interested in finishing. All writers make false starts: a discriminating writer knows what is worth continuing and what is not.

Troubleshooting

Watch out for the students who are always starting something new and never finishing anything. You may need to bring a little subtle pressure to bear on them:

- During a conference, discuss each unfinished piece to find out what the writer's intentions were.
- Show an interest in each piece, ask questions, suggest possibilities. Try to prompt the student to generate more ideas and language.

- At the end of the conference, don't ask whether the student wants to finish any of the pieces. Ask *which one* the student will work on. You are still giving the student some control, but you are limiting the options.

Gently and subtlely, gradually escalate your pressure.

A good principle is:

PROMPT ⟹ **PROD** ⟹ **LEAN**

Rehearsal for Writing

Some students will need time for rehearsal before writing. This rehearsal is a preparation for writing, and can take many forms: talking with a friend, daydreaming, drawing or modeling, dramatic play, reading, researching, interviewing, etc. This is the time for students to ponder topics and approaches, and think through content.

As we have seen, many writers like to have this time to think before actually starting to put words down on paper. They may be silently reliving adventures, retelling anecdotes, creating dialogue, wondering about possible topics and audiences, trying out language, planning a format for presentation.

Young children are usually more impulsive than this. They start with one idea and rush to get it down on paper. Then they are ready to do the same with the next idea. Some experienced writers also like to get pencils in their hands right away, and write as they think. For these writers, the first draft is often less than coherent, being more a series of prompts for the "real" composing to come in the next draft.

The inexperienced writers in our classrooms perhaps do not know yet which kind of writer they are. If they are not given every opportunity and encouragement for different kinds of rehearsal, neither they nor we will ever find out.

Here are some ways you can encourage rehearsal:

- Encourage students to talk to one another about their topics before starting to write.
- Encourage older students to draw or model or role-play before writing. We and they often think this is only appropriate for younger children.
- Have students tell partners what will happen in their stories before they set out to write them.
- Give them plenty of time to browse through research materials before starting to make notes or write reports. They should not be jotting down notes before they have read to the end of the first paragraph of a text.
- Confer with the students before they start to write, to help them verbalize their intentions.
- Encourage the students to write in pairs or small groups. This way they have to talk and make some decisions before they write.

The students must see this rehearsal time as an integral and valued part of the writing process. As with the incubation period, we have to learn not to become too anxious when students appear to be daydreaming!

Troubleshooting

Be aware that for some writers, lengthy or mandatory rehearsal will not be productive. I am one of these writers. I need to write *while* I am thinking out an idea or even a sentence. I do not write sequentially, but in the order I think of things – often from the middle outwards. Afterwards, I look back, see what I have, and decide how to organize it.

Learn who these writers are. They are often the ones whose first drafts are short, messy, crossed out, and incoherent, because they do their organizing in second drafts. Let them work in their own way.

Getting Students to Revise

The craft of writing is learned through revision as the writer focuses on ideas, organization, and language. This is a time to stand back from the writing and look at it through the eyes of a possible reader, to assess how interesting it will be, and how effective in conveying the intended meaning.

Revision should always be a positive experience in which the author tries to improve the piece; it is not an exercise in correcting errors. Revision is time-consuming, often difficult, and rarely fun. If we want our students to do it, we have to make sure that they see a very good reason for it, and that they get some reward at the end of it. This reward is often the appreciative response of an audience when the writing is shared, displayed, or published. When the reward is the satisfaction of the student, then we know we have a writer, not just someone who writes.

Every piece need not be revised. Students should learn that some pieces need more polish than others, and that this is usually determined by the purpose of the writing. Adults know when their writing should be revised and edited; students need to understand this too. You will revise a shopping list, for example, by adding new items as you think of them; but you will not bother to recopy it neatly. On the other hand, when you are sending an important letter and you want to make a good impression, then you will make an extra effort to make the final copy look its best.

Students, especially those who think writing is a one-shot task, need to learn that revision is normal, the way all writers work, the way you expect them to work. I first taught revision in a grade five class. These students had been accustomed for four years to focusing on neatness and spelling at the same time as they were getting their ideas down; one draft was all they had ever done. Their main argument against revision was that it messed up the page!

You can teach students the *principle* of revision without getting them bogged down in time-consuming reworking every time they write:

- Never expect their writing, or your own, to come out right the first time.

- If a student crosses out and changes *one word,* revision has occurred.
- Putting arrows where information is to be moved, or marks to insert new material, is revision, sometimes all that is needed. It takes little time and is not hard work.
- Recopying should not be the inevitable consequence of revision. It is more likely to be the main deterrent. Recopying is for *final draft only*, and should be done only when there will be an audience.

Once the students realize that revision is normal and necessary, you can lead them to make more drastic changes to their work.

I don't like the idea of writing on alternate lines to leave room for changes. This is alright for changing words or correcting spelling. The problem is that it suggests that this is all you ever expect to do. Revisions to content often involve adding and deleting larger amounts of text. Organizational revisions may involve moving whole sentences or paragraphs from one place and inserting them in another. These are the kinds of revisions we want our students to be open to. Such changes will not only make their writing better, but will teach them about composition.

Provide a constructive setting for the students as they revise:

- Make sure each writer always understands the purpose of revision. This usually involves making the writing clearer and more interesting for the reader, or more accurate and satisfying for the writer.
- Encourage students to begin their writing time by rereading what they wrote the day before. By doing this, they may be inspired to continue working on it, rather than starting a new piece every day.
- Do not evaluate first-draft writing, or even comment on spelling or neatness. Teach students that the function of this first draft is to be changed, sometimes to completely disappear or be unrecognizable in the final draft.
- Start small. Any time students add a sentence or choose a better word, they are revising, and learning that this is the normal way writers work.

- Model the revision process when you write on the board, on chart paper, or on the overhead projector. Let the students see words being changed, sentences being discarded and reformulated, information being rearranged, and a new draft being written.
- Allow sufficient time for revision. Never expect writing to be completed in one session.
- Discuss possible revisions during a conference, and make sure the writer understands and *agrees* that they will make the writing better.
- Have the students bring writing that is ready for revision to a group conference. During the conference, help the group to react to the pieces in a constructive way, and to show the writers where revision would make them better/ clearer/more enjoyable.
- Teach the students to use revision shortcuts, such as omission marks and arrows. Teach them to cross out words and sentences they do not want, and explain that clarity and style are more important than neatness in early drafts. Show them how to cut and paste to rearrange sentences or paragraphs, or to insert new information.
- The students should keep all their drafts. When they have finished a piece, have them put their drafts side by side to see how revision made a difference. This is also useful information to send home to parents, to explain what the students are learning.
- With the author's permission, display several drafts of a piece of writing to illustrate the revision process to others.
- Use the overhead projector to display a piece of writing (it could be your own) at a group conference. Have the group work together to make revisions.
- Share your own writing with the children, and follow up on suggestions they make. Let them know that adults don't get it right the first time either; in fact, they never expect to.
- Reward, reinforce, and spread the word when a student makes revisions. Let the children know you value it highly.

Troubleshooting

You will have to lean a little on those students who do not respond to your hints to revise.

You must leave decisions about revision up to the writer. However, you can be subversive in your suggestions. For example, if a student has told you an anecdote which really should be included in a piece of writing, don't say, "Would you like to put that into your story?" Rather say, "Where do you think that story should go in here?" Then suggest they mark the spot with an asterisk.

Publishing is a great motivator. As editor, you will have final say over what is published. Do not accept writing that needs revision. Be honest. Tell the writer the piece does not have enough detail to be interesting, or that the facts are not in a logical order, or that it is not up to that writer's usual standard. Everyone has a reputation to consider!

Remember:

PROMPT ⇨ **PROD** ⇨ **LEAN**

Editing Students' Work

I remember students in my grade five class asking me to edit their writing. In the general course of responding to their writing, I was never one to write all over it – revisions were their job. But when I was asked to edit, I used to do what an editor does. I questioned parts that were not clear, corrected every spelling error, improved on punctuation, indicated where paragraphs should be opened or closed, and generally covered the students' papers in red ink.

And they were grateful!

You see, when they asked me to edit, it was because they were planning to do a final draft, and they had learned that if there were still errors in a final draft it was not final, but needed to be done again. Editing could save them a lot of time and effort. Therefore, they saw editing as a positive, helping strategy. Correction, on the other hand, is usually seen as negative. I have never had a student come and ask me to mark every error in a piece of writing, but many would insist on me doing this kind of editing. What I did would be the same in both cases; the difference was in the perception of the writer. Understanding what it is for makes all the difference.

When writers share or display their work, they usually want to make a good impression on their readers. This is why editing, proofreading, and making a neat final draft are the last stages of the writing process. Our writing is not the best it can possibly be until these things have been done.

We would like our students to be skilled in proofreading and able to correct spelling errors, use conventions of print such as punctuation, and write in a neat hand. These skills are not integral to good composition, except in the sense that the more automatic transcription is, the more a writer can focus on ideas and language, and the more he or she is likely to write. A writer who dictates into a tape recorder and has a secretary transcribe it may never physically put a word on paper. Nevertheless, that person is still a writer.

Composition and transcription are quite different activities. The beauty of teaching writing as a process involving different steps is that we can have our students focus on composing and transcribing at different times. The best chance we have of helping our students become proficient both in composing and in transcribing is to teach them to focus on them one at a time – first do the composing, then concentrate on the spelling, handwriting, punctuation, etc.

Recopying something neatly and correctly is time-consuming and usually boring. It must never be done for its own sake, because it has no purpose other than to make a good impression on someone else. Doing it to learn how it is done may seem valuable to us, but it is not a good motivator for real commitment from students. Students must expect to recopy only when the piece is for an audience. Therefore, we must provide that audience as often as possible, and make sure our students care about the impression they are making on others; no one wants to look bad in front of friends.

Here are a few guidelines for editing:

- Students should do their own first proofreading. Even if they miss most of their errors, practice is the only thing that will hone their skills.
- Working with partners may help students develop their proofreading skills.
- As a general rule, students should be responsible for correcting as much as they know how to do. If they misspell words they know how to spell, or which they can find, they should make the corrections. If they know how to use quotation marks, they should be responsible for putting them in. A list of the things they know how to do could be kept in or on their writing folders.
- The final conference about a piece of writing may provide an opportunity to teach one of the skills of transcription.
- Editing the student cannot yet do should be done by someone else, either you, a volunteer, or another student. Invented spellings should be changed to standard. Punctuation and capitalization should be added. Even if the student does not do it personally, you are still teaching the *principle* that editing must be done. The student will gradually increase the number of things he or she can proofread for and correct.
- The student's words and syntax should not be changed. If sentences are not easily understood, this should be discussed during a conference. The child may then take the opportunity to clarify or rewrite the language. If the language is still not understandable, the child needs to learn this through audience feedback. During your conferences, you can be the first audience, to give the writer a sense of possible audience reaction.
- If possible, some of the students' pieces should be typed. This is particularly useful for those who have difficulty with transcription. Students who cannot make a final draft look beautiful should still have the pride of authorship.

Troubleshooting

Some students cannot find their errors when they proofread. This may be because they have not yet learned a particular skill. In this case, it is not a problem; they will learn in time.

Sometimes older students who are poor spellers cannot recognize whether a spelling is right or wrong. Some people will go through adulthood not being able to proofread and correct their errors. This can present problems which adults have to learn to compensate for. (They either do not write, or they have someone else check their writing for them. I know one adult who cultivates illegible handwriting to cover up possible spelling mistakes.)

The biggest problem for these students in school is that they may draw the conclusion that because they cannot be accurate spellers, they are poor writers. They may be unwilling to write for fear of making mistakes. These students know that they have a problem, and that they will have to learn to deal with it. We need to teach them coping strategies.

You can help by teaching them three things:

- Editing is important. It is essential for a final draft, whether the student or someone else does it.
- There will generally be someone who will do for the students, without penalty or shame, what they are unable to do themselves. Therefore there is no reason not to write.
- At the appropriate time, the students will be helped to increase their own skill level.

Using a Computer

Any child who can recognize letters can write with a computer. In fact it is particularly useful for beginners; it is much easier to recognize a "B" than to remember how to make one. Also, children who do not yet have control over printing can produce text which looks perfect to them; suddenly they can read what they have written – and so can we. Older students need to be able to type quickly enough that their thought stream is not slowed to a halt; it is hard to think creatively one word at a time. Perhaps we will need to reassess at what point we teach keyboarding.

The benefits of the computer for editing are obvious. A writer is apt to be more of a perfectionist when changes can be made easily, when menial tasks can be performed quickly. Manipulation of text can be almost a pleasure. Many teachers input students' work at final-draft stage so that the students can work on word choice, paragraphing, spelling, punctuation, etc. There is nothing wrong with this. However, to gain the full benefit from the computer we need to teach our students that it is more than a fancy typewriter. Its real benefit is as a composing machine.

Risk-taking is a prerequisite for successful writing. In fact it is a necessary part of all learning. Many students are hesitant to try out new ideas and techniques, sometimes to put pen to paper at all, because they are afraid of making mistakes. No one wants to look silly in print. The computer invites risk-taking, because the writer has total control over what will appear ultimately on the paper and what will be instantly erased. Students can soon learn that their writing will not be printed until they say it is finished–when it is the best they can make it. Unlike speech, writing is not irrevocable. Once you have spoken, you cannot recall your words, but writing does not go on public view until the writer says it is ready. When a writer has this power, writing is no longer such a risky business.

Once composition is complete, students can experiment with all the print and design possibilities of their computer program. Whether this is simply choosing type size and style or learning desk-top publishing, students can focus on the presentation of their writing.

Using a computer can be highly motivating for many children. (Some of my students spent longer and longer on writing just so they could retain control of the machine.) The computer can help to teach them about the writing process. Once they have learned that text can be manipulated, that they have control over their final product, this knowledge is likely to stay with them even when the computer is not available. After all, the computer is only a tool. Anything a word-processor will do can also be done with a pencil and a pair of scissors. What will make a difference is the writer's understanding of how to go about the task, and commitment to producing the best product possible.

Recognizing Different Writing Types

Just as adults have different approaches to the writing process, so do children. Some writers pre-rehearse in their minds before they put anything on paper. Much of their organizing, planning, and composing is done in the head before any words are put on paper – in effect, the first draft is done mentally. For these people, the writing may come out quite detailed and "clean". Other people compose as they write. The first effort may be sketchy; it may need to have details added, and other changes made.

We have to be able to recognize which students pre-rehearse, and which compose on the run. They are both valid and effective ways of working, but knowing which style a student favors can alter our expectations, our conference approach, and our evaluation of the work.

For the student who pre-composes mentally, we might be of most help at this stage, rather than waiting until the draft is written. It might be more difficult for this student to see a need for any revision at all, when the writing comes out looking detailed and organized. We must guard against thinking that this student is necessarily the more proficient writer, just because the first draft looks better.

The student who does little pre-composing may produce a first draft that is short, messy, incomplete, and disorganized. The danger here is that the student may think this is a sign of a poor writer. It is vital that this student understand what this first draft is, and that it is a normal way for many people to produce good writing. This student needs to learn as soon as possible that with reflection and revision, this first draft can evolve into a competent, possibly superior piece of writing.

When we evaluate, the final draft, not the first one, is what we should look at. The first draft can teach us about a student's style of composition, and about how much of transcription is automatic, but will not necessarily indicate that student's ability to compose, generate language, and organize information. After all, a good writer is not someone who gets it right the first time, but one who is prepared to work at it until it is the best it can possibly be.

Each student should be encouraged to use whichever style produces the best results.

Writer's Block

Every writer, at some time or another, will have dry periods, will try to avoid writing, will become discouraged. You will see these different writing moods in your students. At such times writers might need a little extra help and encouragement, but blocks should not necessarily be seen as problems, either by you or by the students concerned. Everyone should see varying degrees of motivation and satisfaction as normal facets of writing.

As you observe your students at work, you might watch for signs of non-productive behaviors. Don't be in too much of a hurry to step in, though. Often a student just needs time to sort out problems and get back on track. However, if some students seem to fall into a prolonged, negative pattern, then you should offer some help. Here are some behaviors you might observe, and some strategies which could change them:

The writer seems to be in a dry period.

- Ask the student what he or she thinks is the cause of the problem.
- Help the student generate a list of possible writing topics. Then ask the student which one he or she will try first.
- Get the student to work with a partner. The partner may generate ideas which the two can work on together.
- Consider moving the student towards a different kind of writing. Perhaps there are letters to write, records to keep, signs to put up.

The student constantly has trouble getting started on a piece of writing. This could be due to a number of causes:

- The student does not like to write.
  In this case, you should think seriously about the context

for the writing: if the writing serves no valid purpose for the student, then he or she will not be able to do it, even if willing to try. This student needs to have more control over the purpose and content of the writing. Perhaps the tasks could be smaller, the rewards more frequent.

- The student is afraid of making mistakes.
  For this student, you must make an extra effort to focus only on content, and not on style, words, or presentation.
- The student thinks you always have to start with a good first sentence, but he or she can't get the words to come out right. This student might do better by listing ideas and words, or by starting with an easier part of the writing. There is no reason why the first paragraph has to be written first – it is often the hardest part to write.

The student never seems to finish a piece.

- The student may not be clear about why he or she is doing the writing in the first place. Perhaps there needs to be a definite audience or recipient in view from the beginning.
- Perhaps the student has a low opinion of the writing, and does not see how to make it successful. With this student, you need to point out the strengths of the work, and help with organizing them.
- Perhaps the student associates finishing with having a lot of editing, correcting, and recopying to do. This student needs a secretary from time to time to help with the slug work.
- Do not make a rule that everything must be finished. Some writing does not work out, and should be abandoned. Just help children to see which pieces are worth working on, and then help them make them better.
- There is nothing as motivating for a writer as a finished piece of writing that is well received by an audience. If a student cannot finish something alone, he or she could work with a partner or group to produce a polished piece of writing that can be shared or displayed. Once the rewards of authorship have been experienced, the student may be more inclined to strive for a repeat performance.

The student writes on the same topic all the time.

- If a student knows a lot about a subject, it is natural to want to write about it a lot. If one has specialized knowledge, it can help make one's writing more interesting and deep. This has worked very well for authors like Dick Francis. On the other hand, the student may be sticking with a safe subject rather than branching out and taking risks with something new. If the writing is repetitive, discuss it with the student, and find out why. Then maybe you can help choose new topics or styles.

- Young children who are anxious about spelling correctly often write by using only the words they know how to spell. When they know only a handful of words, this makes the writing difficult and repetitive, not to mention boring. You need to break their dependence on having the spellings correct in a first draft. Do not give them spellings when they ask you; tell them to write the sounds they hear, and you will help them with the spellings later. Then, when the writing is finished, give them any spellings they ask you for. Make sure you do not praise them for good spelling or printing during first-draft writing – this will only reinforce their false notions about what they are supposed to focus on.

When your students are experiencing a dry period, or are not having much success, try to help them, but also make sure they know that all writers have the same problems. It is no good trying to teach them that writing is always fun, or that they should always be equally successful at it; it won't happen that way. Just as we have to be patient with them, they must learn to be patient with themselves, and not expect instant success. Writing isn't that easy.

4
AUDIENCE AWARENESS

Developing a Sense of Audience

When I was in school, the only audience for my writing was the teacher. The teacher always responded in the same mode, letting me know how well or poorly I had done the work. Every piece of writing was for the same audience, and it elicited the same response – evaluation. Each piece of writing was a test. And let's not kid ourselves that anyone ever learned anything by taking a test!

Having a sense of audience can help a writer to step outside the writing and look at it from a neutral corner. This is a first step towards learning how to make the writing better. A writer needs to know that different audiences require different styles of writing: *Readers' Digest* writing is not like *Time* writing; writing to a teenage friend is not like writing to an adult relative. As we have seen, one of the important questions a writer must ask is, "Who is the writing for?"

In order to develop a sense of audience, writers need different kinds of response to their writing. You can give them many kinds of audience:

Themselves
- Journals, notes, and first drafts may have only the writer as audience.
- The author may review several pieces of writing to decide which to read at a group conference, which piece to discuss with you, or which piece to revise for possible publication.

- A writer may review the work at any stage and focus on any aspect that is relevant at the time.

An Interested Adult
- This might be you, a classroom volunteer, or a parent.
- The aim is to respond to the content in an interested and supportive way, as you would in a conversation.
- This response may come at any time during the production of a piece of writing.
- This kind of response tends to focus on content, rather than style.

A Partner in Dialogue
- This is likely to be you, particularly at conference time.
- The partner's role is to help the writer see the writing from a different perspective.
- The partner will discuss ideas, ask questions, offer suggestions, help solve problems, and respond in a constructive way.
- This response can be at any time before, while, or after the writing is done.
- This response may be to any or all of the processes and skills involved in writing.

Peers
- This response might be elicited through a group conference.
- Peers can also help while collaborating on a piece of writing.
- Classmates' response is gained through sharing, publishing, or displaying finished work or work in progress.
- Feedback on ideas and strategies should be ongoing throughout the writing.

Outside Audience
- This might be the recipient of a letter, the reader of a school magazine, a student in another class who reads another student's published book, or a passerby reading a bulletin board.

- Because the audience is unknown, and possibly unfamiliar, more demands are placed on the writer. More dispassionate reflection and appraisal are needed.
- This response comes after the writing is finished, when the writer has in effect said, "This is the best I can do." It is final-draft feedback.

Each of these situations has the potential to give students a different kind of response, and therefore a different perspective on writing.

Classroom Publishing

Classroom publishing provides one kind of purpose and audience for the students' writing, and a valid reason for revising and editing.

You could work with each student to select a suitable piece during a writing conference. During the selection process, the writer should be considering the piece with regard to the intended format and audience. The piece chosen might go through further revision at this point.

If a student asks that a particular piece be published, you should then act as editor, discussing with the student anything that still needs to be done with the piece to get it ready for publishing. If you maintain high standards, you will give the students a goal to work for in their revising, editing, and presentation.

As a general rule, you might try to publish or display one piece per student per month, or as close to that as you can manage. Some might be individual books, others could be group or class collaborative writing, or anthologies of stories or poems. Some students may want every piece to be published. This is not a good idea. For one thing, you do not have the time to do it. More important, publishing and sharing should be seen as something one does only with the very best work, not with everything one writes. It is a celebration of special writing, not a regular routine. This is the way it is in the real world.

You might set up a special place to store and display student-authored books, where they are available for general reading as part of the classroom library.

Planning for Publishing

There are a number of decisions to be made before a book can be prepared for publishing. Ask the student to make these decisions. Doing so will allow the writer to retain full control of the finished product, and will also teach the student that final-draft writing involves planning and organizing.

Here are some of the questions you may need to ask:

- "How many pages will you need?" To decide this, the student should go through the text and mark where each new page will start.
- "What size will the pages be?"
- "Will you print the text, or should it be typed?" If it is to be typed, any instructions to the typist should be written on the text.
- "Will there be a title page? End pages? A dedication?"
- "Will there be illustrations? Where will they be? Will they be full pages?" The student should write a note in the text where illustrations will be, and make sure they are added to the page count.
- "What kind of cover will the book need? Hard cover? Soft cover? An illustrated cover?"

Troubleshooting

Children should not start writing a first draft directly into a folded and stapled pre-made booklet. This will make them think that writing a finished piece is a one-shot operation, and this is not what we want to teach. A book must be a final draft, as good and polished as it can possibly be. Even the youngest children can learn this. Any misunderstandings they develop about writing and how it is done will have to be unlearned later, and this is very difficult, sometimes impossible to do.

Hints on Bookbinding

Soft Cover

Fold together the right number of blank pages for the book. Print and illustrate the book, starting on the first right-hand page.

Use bristol board for the cover. Have the child print the title and do any cover illustrating. Cut the cover to be slightly larger than the printed pages. Fold over; stitch or staple the pages through the centre fold.

Hard Cover

Fold together the right number of blank pages for the book. Print and illustrate the book, starting on the first right hand page.

Add one extra folded blank page as beginning and ending pages. Stitch or staple through the centre fold.

Make the cover. Cut two pieces of stiff cardboard (carton) slightly larger than a single page of the book. Place them side by side on wallpaper or fabric, leaving a narrow space between the two inside edges. Cut the wallpaper or fabric five centimetres larger all round. Fold the edges in over the cardboard, and stick them down with strong glue.

Paste the blank beginning and end pages to the inside of the cover.

Larger Format Laminated Books

These books take longer to build, and require more materials, but they arc very attractive and stand up to many readings. There is also no limit to the size of page you can use, as long as you can get it into your laminating machine. (If you have a laminating press, rather than a roller, you can use more than one pressing per page.) This method is more suitable for group or class collaborative books, as you won't have time to do it very often.

Have the students prepare all the pages for the book, with text and illustrations. Number the pages in order.

Cut construction paper big enough to leave at least a one-centimetre border round the edges. Glue the book pages on both sides of this construction paper. Laminate the pages, and trim the edges.

Make a strong cover by putting a layer of construction paper over each side of a sheet of bristol board. Cut the bristol board one centimetre larger than the pages of the book. Paste the cover title and illustration on the front, and a similar piece on the back cover. Laminate the cover, and trim the edges.

Now fasten the cover and pages together. Place the cover and first page side by side, as if the book is open to page one. Run a strip of transparent tape down the join. Turn the page. Put the second page in place, and run a strip of tape down the join. Continue until you have glued all the pages, and the back cover. (You don't need to use invisible tape. It will disappear anyway because of the lamination.)

Finally, use heavy bookbinding tape to cover the spine.

Troubleshooting

Stitched books stand up better than stapled books to repeated readings and handlings. Construction paper needs to be laminated before it is stitched; otherwise it rips easily.

If you use a standard page size (e.g., 8 1/2" x 7"), you, your volunteer, or your students can take an hour from time to time and make a stack of book covers, so you have one whenever you need it.

Sometimes, you will find that you get behind in your publishing. Don't worry about this. I had one box labeled "Stories for Typing" and another labeled "Books for Binding". Sometimes work would sit in the box until I or a parent volunteer was able to get around to it. This is alright. Publishing is not an instant operation in the professional world either. Students need to know that typing, illustrating, and binding books is time-comsuming work. The finished book will be even more special, cared for, and valued as a result.

Fostering a Sense of Authorship

We want our students to think of themselves as writers, not just as children learning to write. Everything we learned about language we learned not by being taught about it, but by using it to do things. There was never a time in our lives when we thought of ourselves as children practising talking and listening; we just talked and listened in order to get along in our everyday lives. The more involved we were in the world of language around us, and the more we tried to join in, the more we improved in our ability to make language work for us.

We used to have a saying in teaching, that first we learn to read, then we read to learn. This is an odd way of looking at learning. Would we say, for example, that first we learn to talk, then we talk to communicate? Or first we learn to listen, then we listen to understand? We know language learning does not work this way. The idea that you can learn to read before actually doing real reading is as silly as believing that you can learn to talk and listen before communicating and understanding meaning.

The same thing is true of writing. We do not learn to write first, then do real writing; it all happens at the same time. It is the need to communicate that drives the learning. Our students will develop as writers as they write for real purposes and real audiences.

Pride in authorship is probably the greatest motivator there is when it comes to getting students to write and to develop as writers. We have taken the first step in creating authors when we publish their work. Here are some other ways you can foster this growing sense of authorship:

- Raise the children's awareness of the authors of the books they read. Sometimes they don't realize that real people have worked to produce these books. From time to time, choose an "Author of the Week". This might be the author of a book, story, or poem the students are reading in class. You could from time to time also have an "Illustrator of the Week", and look at styles of artwork. (For more about such events, see "Studying Other Authors and Illustrators" in Chapter 5.)

- Give the students' writing the same status as professional writing. Have their books in the classroom library for general reading. From time to time, choose one of them for your read-aloud time.
- Encourage the students to add author biographies and photographs to their own published books.
- Encourage the students to ask the same questions about the professionally written books they read as they ask one another about their own writing. Critical reading is the same skill, no matter who the author is. In this way, students can see links between reading and writing. After all, they are reading writing, and writing reading. The more they know about one, the better they will understand the other.
- If possible, have a professional author visit the class. Even if you can't find a novelist or a poet, you can often get a reporter from your local paper. Even unpublished authors can give the students insights into the processes, the joys and frustrations of writing. It is quite revealing for the students to find out that professional writers have the same problems and work in the same way they do.
- Have your students visit other classes, taking along their own books to share. They can then be visiting authors and talk about their own writing experiences.
- Have a regular "Story Circle" time. In a story circle, students who choose to can take turns to read aloud a piece they have chosen and rehearsed. To make sure they rehearse, post a sign-up sheet a couple of days beforehand, and have students write their names and the pieces they will read. They may read something they have authored, a professionally written story, or a student-authored book from the classroom library.
- Make sure that every student has published work in the classroom. For some students, this may mean having them participate in a group writing experience. Students who have trouble transcribing neatly will need to have someone else print or type their books. They, too, should have pride in authorship of a beautiful book.

- As a special event, once a year, hold a school or district "Writers' Festival" as a way to celebrate young authors. Here are some events you could feature:
    - Invite professional writers and illustrators to talk to groups of students.
    - Set up displays of published student writing.
    - Organize workshops to teach students specific skills such as bookbinding, illustrating, making endpages, cartooning, etc.
    - Order jacket patches saying "WRITER" for students who have published work.
    - Have "Readers' Circles" at which students who wish to can read aloud from their own work, published or unpublished.

5
LEARNING FROM OTHER PEOPLE

Modeling the Process

When I began to teach grade one, I was very conscious that my blackboard writing was not the easiest to read. I still wrote in the English style, and was not used to printing at all. And I got only C for "Blackboard" in teachers' college. Consequently I made a special effort with my balls and sticks, and tried to be as neat and exact as I could. It was some time before I realized that what I was demonstrating was that when I wrote, it always came out right the first time.

If we want our students to know that writing is a process, that revising and editing, and making a mess, and having problems, and getting things wrong are natural parts of writing, we must demonstrate these things for them.

You can model the process through many everyday writing opportunities in which you are acting as scribe and the students are watching you. The children can see how writing develops as you record on chart paper, chalkboard, or overhead projector:

- experience chart stories
- group compositions
- lists, charts
- letters
- announcements, instructions, etc.

The students can see the process at work if you do some of the following:

- Treat any initial recording as a draft. Do all you can to show that the final form is not important yet. Don't take any special effort with handwriting or printing. If you make a mistake, don't erase it – cross it out. Don't do any fancy decoration at this stage. If the students can't read it easily, don't worry; the important thing at this stage is that the writer can read it. (This can be very liberating.)

- As you write, or during a rereading of what you have written, add, delete, or rearrange information, words, sentences, or whole paragraphs. Do this by crossing out, writing above the line, using omission marks, or drawing arrows to indicate where information is to be moved.
- Think and question aloud while you are writing.
  For example:

  "I wonder if we need to say a little more about this?"
  "I think this would make more sense down here."
  "I'm not sure how to spell this; I'll make a note and look it up later."
  "I wonder if this is the best word?"

- Write a second draft after revisions have been made. Don't take it home to make it neat – do it while the students are watching, or busy with other work.
- Use correct "authoring" terminology: first draft, revising, editing, second draft, final draft, publishing (this "jargon" will also give you and the students "author language" for conferences).

When the children see you modeling writing in this way, they will begin to understand that no one expects writing to come out right the first time. It will prove to them that you really mean what you say. It is natural for them to copy what they see the adults around them doing; they will likely apply the same principles to their own writing.

Studying Other Authors and Illustrators

In their reading, the students will have encountered different authors, illustrators, and styles and formats of writing. Some of the children may have spontaneously begun to borrow ideas, patterns, and formats for their own writing. You can foster this developing awareness of authoring by doing some of the following:

- Point out the names of authors and illustrators of material the children are reading.
- Provide other material by the same authors and illustrators. In this way the students may become aware of a particular author's style, kinds of subject matter, language, etc.
- Discuss similarities and differences in topics, forms, etc.
- Compare and contrast styles of illustrations. Talk about why an illustrator might have chosen a particular technique or style.
- Use patterns from literature for group/individual writing. (See "Using Literary Patterns", below.)
- Talk about *your* favorite authors and illustrators.

As noted earlier, one special event in the classroom could be an "Author/Illustrator of the Week". You might choose the author or illustrator of a story the students are reading. Or you might have a special read-aloud book to share. Here are some of the activities that could be part of an "Author/Illustrator of the Week" event.

- Set up a display of works by the author/illustrator you have chosen. You could collect them with the help of your librarian, or have a few of the students search them out.
- Give a book talk. Share parts of several books and invite the students to read them for themselves.
- Invite students who wish to to write a story of their own in the style of the chosen author, or about some favorite characters, or a sequel or additional adventure or anecdote. They could do this individually or in small groups. Set aside a time for them to share their stories, either with the whole class or in small groups.
- Hold a story circle. Students who wish to can practise and read aloud a favorite story or excerpt from the chosen author. Put up a sign-up sheet a couple of days ahead of your story circle, so the students have plenty of time to practise what they have chosen. Choose one student to be chairperson, to announce each reading and keep things

moving. Gather all the chairs in a circle, or set up a reader's chair at the front of the group.

- If a story consists mostly of dialogue with some narration, the students could work in small groups to read it aloud like a play. This gives them opportunities for rereading and rehearsal before their oral performance. They could present their reading as a puppet play, or record it as a radio play for the listening centre, if you have one.

Troubleshooting

Be careful about students presenting unscripted plays. These often turn into dramatic play, which might be fine for the participants, but can drag on and get very boring for an audience. Also, you don't want a few students to monopolize the time with readings that are too long. To avoid this, you might set a time limit. If you limit any presentation or reading to five minutes you will force students to rehearse, and ensure that many children have a chance to participate. Use an oven-timer with a bell, and have your chairperson set it before each presentation. This may seem arbitrary, but your students will get used to the amount of time they should plan for, and will accept the impartial restriction.

Using Literary Patterns

As students read more and more, they will become used to the language of literature. Even very young children know that literary language is in many ways unlike the language they speak. For example, the nursery rhymes and nonsense skipping rhymes they chant are loved and repeated more for their sounds and rhythms than for their deeper meanings. Children often put on special sing-song voices for this kind of chant, and very young children often learn the rhythm and intonation of a rhyme before they know the words.

As the students become more familiar with the language of literature, this language can become a resource for their own writing. They can learn new forms, experiment with sentence patterns, play with words, and manipulate language to suit their own needs. These patterns can become a structure on which the children can hang their own ideas.

There are a number of different kinds of patterns you can encourage your students to use. For example:

• *Language Patterning*
The children may notice a particular use of language, such as alliteration.
They may use a repeated sentence pattern: "I wish I could ..."

• *Idea Patterning*
They may use a concept from a story they have read, and write it from their own point of view.
For example: "Would you rather ..."(from *Would You Rather* by John Burningham), or "These are a few of my favorite things" (from the song of the same name).

• *Story Patterning*
They could try their own versions of stories they have read, such as fables or fairy tales, or books like *The Snowy Day*, by Ezra Jack Keats.

• *Author Patterning*
They could try out the format, style, and subject matter of a favorite author.

Whichever patterning you choose to use, you can help your students develop their ideas by leading them through the following process:

• *Brainstorming*
List as many ideas as you can about your chosen topic – words, phrases, characters, happenings, rhymes, etc.

• *Selecting*
Choose the best and most compatible of the ideas from your brainstorming.

- *Assembling*
  Put your ideas together.

- *Refining*
  Read over what you have written and see where the ideas, style, or language could be improved.

- *Completing*
  Decide what you will do with the writing, and put it in an appropriate finished form.

This process should be extended over a number of sessions. Don't rush things. You and your students will get better results if you do the following:

- Give ideas time to incubate and develop. List the ideas on chart paper, and leave it posted for the students to add to as they think of new ideas.
- If you are developing ideas with small groups, let them support each other. For example, one group might do the brainstorming, another group could add ideas. A third group could do some selecting, and a fourth group start putting the ideas together. At each stage, the different groups could enter into a dialogue about the decisions being made. Each group will then be involved in critical review of the work so far, making decisions about revision, and contributing new ideas.

Collaborating

Children are used to collaborating in much of what they do. They build, play games, investigate their environment, solve problems, and make plans together. Much of their spoken language is developed through interaction with their friends and classmates.

There is much to be gained by encouraging your students to collaborate in their writing, either in pairs, or in small groups of three or four:

- As they compose together, they verbalize thoughts, build on each other's ideas, create dialogue, and generate language. They cannot do the job without talk so planning, problem-solving, and decision-making are built-in parts of collaborating.

- Writing can be an extension of children's dramatic play. The play is essentially a composing activity, which can grow naturally into collaborative writing.
- Writing pieces may become longer and more detailed. As we have seen, one of the difficulties of writing is that it is like a monologue, and can be hard to maintain. It is usually easier to sustain a dialogue than a monologue.
- As they talk through their ideas, students constantly improve on and extend their partners' ideas and language. Spontaneous revision is taking place as they go, and this may help them see writing as something to be worked out and manipulated.
- The children often enjoy working together, and consequently take more pleasure in writing.
- The children may divide the tasks: one may print or write while the other illustrates; they may share in the researching and reference work. This makes some of the time-consuming routine tasks of writing and editing more manageable.
- Some students think of themselves as poor writers, not because they have no ideas, but because they have trouble getting them down on paper. Having partners to act as scribes can enable these children to see just how many ideas and how much language they do have when they can focus on composition alone.

Here are a few ways you can provide opportunities for students to collaborate in writing:

- Draw their attention to books they read which have more than one author, or a different author and illustrator. Show them that in the world beyond school tasks are often shared.
- Have them do lots of brainstorming in small groups. All group members contribute ideas, but only one does the recording.
- When students are doing research projects, encourage them to work in pairs or small groups. Give them plenty

of time for planning, sharing, discussing, and organizing their research and writing.

- Make it easy for them to work together during their personal writing time. Talk to partners or groups together during conference time.
- Offer your own services from time to time as scribe for students having trouble getting their ideas down on paper. Show them that there are times when their ideas are all that matter.
- Provide frequent opportunities for small group composing with you as the scribe. During these sessions you can guide the composing, encourage discussion, do as much changing as the students dictate, and help them work through the writing process.
- Establish a reasonable level of talk as a normal part of the workshop atmosphere in the writing period.

Troubleshooting

If it seems to you that some students tend to be passive listeners in group writing, don't worry too much. This does not necessarily mean they are not learning anything. They will be part of the interaction of other group members, whether they say anything or not. To give these students a greater opportunity to contribute, you might want to make sure that they work often with just one partner.

Often you will find that the same students always do the recording. This may be because they are more willing, because they write faster and more neatly, or because they are the better spellers. Don't worry about this. These children may need to feel that they are experts in something. The others will have other opportunities during the day to practise their own handwriting and record their own thoughts and ideas.

6
EXPANDING THE STUDENTS' REPERTOIRE

Modes of Writing

All writing is not the same. Writing a poem is not like writing a story; writing an essay is not like writing a list of instructions. Because a person can do one kind of writing well, it does not necessarily follow that he or she will be good at all kinds of writing

In school, it is not only important that students do a lot of writing; it is also important that they do many different kinds of writing.

If we are to provide instruction and opportunities for our students, it is important for us to know what different kinds of writing they need to do. Here is one way of categorizing language in modes which can be very useful when planning classroom writing experiences.[*]

- Expressive
- Transactional
- Poetic

Much writing is a combination of these modes, which I will explain in more detail below. However, for the writer, each piece of writing tends to have a focus in one mode or another.

The different modes make different demands on writers. When you are planning classroom writing experiences, you might find it helpful to keep different modes in mind, so you can make sure the students are experiencing all three.

An immature or inexperienced writer, of any age, is likely to function better in the expressive mode. Also, when we are

[*]*The Development of Writing Abilities (11-18)* by James Britton et al. London: Macmillan, 1975.

writing about a subject we do not fully understand yet, or are thinking through new ideas and concepts, the expressive mode is likely to give us our best chance of success. As our children become more experienced as writers, our job will be to broaden their use of language to include more transactional and poetic writing.

Here are some things you can do to help students develop their range as writers:

- Provide models of the kind of writing you want them to learn about. It is hard to write a recipe if you have never seen one.
- Teach them the special requirements of each task: how to make notes; when a list is better than a paragraph; how to organize a report.
- Encourage them to use expressive writing in various subject areas. Writing about science or history in the expressive mode will enable them to think through new ideas and explain them in their own terms.
- Remember that they will need a lot of practice to become proficient. They need to keep revisiting the kinds of writing they have learned about.

Troubleshooting

When you evaluate student writing, bear in mind the mode of writing being used, and the student's experience with it. Remember that transactional and poetic writing make more demands on the writer than purely expressive writing. First efforts will likely not be completely successful. Look for ways in which they are successful, and parts the students need help with.

Expressive Writing

When young children first start to write, their work is most likely to be talk written down. They write about themselves: what they do, what they think, what happens to them, what is important to them. Their written language is much like their spoken language.

As we get older, we still keep this kind of writing for certain occasions. Personal letters, diaries and journals, messages, and so on tend to be written in expressive language. Any kind of stream-of-consciousness writing is likely to be expressive.

In expressive writing we still tend to write about ourselves and what is important to us. We are always at the centre. We are not writing for any audience except ourselves and people close to us, people we know well. We are not trying to impress, just to be ourselves. Because we are using our own most familiar language and style, this kind of writing is relatively easy to do.

Since expressive writing is so close to our own thoughts and language, it is most likely to be the mode we use to frame new thoughts and ideas, to solve problems, and to understand new concepts. It is the language of learning and exploring, of writing to find out what we think and to organize our ideas.

Give your students plenty of opportunities to use the expressive mode:

- Allow as much time as possible for personal writing. When students have choice and control, they frequently use expressive writing.
- Have them start personal response journals in which they can record their thoughts, ideas, and impressions. They could focus on their response to books they are reading, or their thoughts, problems, and predictions about topics they are working on in math, science, or history.
- Give expressive mode assignments in various subjects. For example, ask the students to retell a history "happening" by writing it as if they were participants, or to explain what happened in a science experiment in their own words, rather than in a formal report.
- Set up classroom mail slots to encourage the exchange of letters and notes. You can make these by taping together several liquor-bottle cartons with the dividers still in them. (You will need to reinforce the sections with bookbinding tape.) Have slots for the students, teachers who work in the room, volunteers, and frequent visitors. Add a slot for external mail to other classrooms.

Transactional Writing

Transactional writing is the kind that gets jobs done. It is the language of reports, instructions, and records. Its main function is to record and transmit information and facts.

When you read an auto-repair manual, you are not too concerned with the author's view of the world, only on whether he or she has the facts straight. In transactional writing, getting the facts right is important; truth and accuracy matter. It is also important that the information is complete, with no vital points left out. Not only that, the information needs to be organized in a way that makes it easy for the reader to understand.

A recipe is a good example of transactional writing:

- It has a particular format which is unlike other kinds of writing; all recipes tend to look the same, and you know what to expect in them.
- It has its own special technical terms and ways of using language (baste, pinch, cream, etc.).
- It presents bits of information in the order in which you need them.
- It sometimes has pictures or diagrams to help you make sure you are doing things right.
- You read it for a specific purpose, to do a specific job; you do not usually read it for entertainment.
- Everyone who reads and follows it should finish up with the same information and product.

Because of these special needs, transactional writing can be harder to do than expressive writing. Anyone who has had to assemble something by following written instructions knows that if the writing is not well executed, it can cause tremendous problems.

There will be many opportunities for transactional writing in your classroom:

- Putting up signs and notices
- Writing a timetable or schedule
- Leaving messages
- Making lists of things to do
- Making notes on a research topic
- Recording observations from a science experiment

- Writing a research report
- Recording steps to solve a math problem
- Recording ideas during brainstorming
- Making plans
- Drawing up maps, charts, and graphs
- Writing letters for information
- Answering questions

Poetic Writing

Poetic writing is the language of literature. It is language in its most polished form, writing designed for an audience, writing that stands as an art form in itself.

In poetic writing what matters most is the impact the writing has on the reader. Will the reader laugh and cry at the right moments? Truth and accuracy are less important than whether the words convey the mood and spirit the author wants.

People who write advertising copy really understand poetic writing. They are experts in audience impact. Many advertisements do not persuade you to buy by presenting the bare facts about a product; they want to create images in the mind of the reader. They use a minimum of time and space to get across their message; every second and every word are carefully weighed to produce the desired response. We call it "lifestyle advertising". It is often criticized because it is so powerful, and therefore successful.

Because poetic writing always has the reader in mind, because it requires control and power over language, it is also more demanding on the writer than expressive writing.

Make sure your students have many opportunities for poetic writing by:

- Patterning from literature
- Preparing writing for display or publication
- Reading their own writing aloud in a story circle
- Taking part in editing conferences about other students' writing
- Brainstorming words and phrases
- Listening to the sound of words, as well as considering their meaning

- Writing poetry
- Focusing on the words they choose to convey meanings and moods

Making the Writing Better

We have accepted the idea that writing does not usually come out in its best form in one draft. A large part of what a writer does is to take whatever comes out in a first draft and work on it to make it better.

In order to make revisions, a writer needs to read the first draft critically and evaluate it from the standpoints of purpose and audience – in other words, to go back to the two questions all writers must ask themselves when they sit down to write:

- What is it for?
- Who is it for?

To make an evaluation of his or her work, the writer must ask questions like the following:

- Does this piece accomplish what I set out to do?
- Will my readers be able to understand what I am saying?
- Is this the best I can do with this piece?

Because revision involves being a critical reader of a piece of writing, it may be the best way to teach students how to make their writing better.

Helping students to reflect on purpose and audience – and how well they are meeting their demands – during the process of writing may be helpful. When you talk to students about a piece of writing in progress, you might focus their attention with questions and statements such as these:

About Purpose
- "Why are you doing this piece of writing?"
- "What are you planning to do with it?"
- "Who do you want to read it when you are done?"

About Content
- "What are you writing about?"
- "What is the most important thing you want me to learn from this paragraph?"

- "I don't understand what you are saying here. Can you explain it in a different way?"
- "I'm surprised you didn't write more about _____ . I know it's a subject you know a lot about."
- "Is there anything you need to know more about?"
- "Is there anything you would like help with?"

About Organization

- "You seem to have things a little mixed up here. What do you think should come first?"
- "I'm not sure this is the best order for your information. What do you think?"
- "Do you think it might be clearer if you divided this up into sections?"
- "You haven't organized this into paragraphs yet. Do you know how to do that?"
- "Have you thought about putting this information into a list, rather than a paragraph?"
- "What do you think you ought to do next?"
- "Is there anything you would like help with?"

About Style

- "You seem to be using this word over and over again. Can you think of any other words you could use instead?"
- "Did you consider writing this as a diary/letter/play? Do you think it might be effective that way?"
- "You haven't used any dialogue. Was there any special reason for this?"
- "Is there anything you need help with?"

About Presentation

- "Do you know how to head a letter?"
- "Have you thought about how you will present this to the group? Will you put up a poster? Read it aloud?"

The stage the writing is at will indicate to you which area to focus on. If you want to refresh your memory, reread the section on "The Structure of a Conference" in Chapter 2.

Teacher-Directed Writing

Skill as a writer is not a matter of how much writing you can do. What is more important is how many ways you can make writing work for you.

When your students are free to make all the choices in their personal writing time, you may find that many of them use a limited range of modes, styles, and formats. Some of them always write personal anecdotes; some never write anything personal. Some of them make up stories; others do not. A few of them write on the same topic over and over again. This is usually alright. They will be choosing topics they have a desire and a need to write about, formats they know how to use, and styles they are comfortable with.

As students develop in their ability to use written language, we want to expand their repertoire. We want them to learn new ways of creating, explaining, describing, recording, manipulating language, and organizing information. Personal writing will not provide enough opportunities for this. To make sure the students use many kinds of language and techniques, we need another component in our writing program.

You may look at your classroom writing opportunities as a two-part program:

1. Personal Writing

This will likely be a regular time each day when the students have full control over the writing they do. They will have their own purposes, choose their own topics, decide on format and style, and make decisions about revising, editing, sharing, and publishing. Your role is to be an interested partner in the writing task, provide initial audience reaction, help students develop their topics, and teach them specific skills they need – in general, to take whatever it is they are trying to do and help them do it better.

2. Teacher-Directed Writing

This is any writing you assign. It may take the form of:
- A personal response to literature

- Research notes and a report
- Recording observations
- Patterning from literature
- Trying out a particular form of poetry writing
- A journal or log entry
- A group-composing activity

By assigning specific writing tasks, you can ensure that the students have many opportunities to use different modes of writing. This is not a substitute for personal writing; it is a necessary complement to it. As you widen the students' experience in different ways to use written language, they will have more techniques to choose from and use in their personal writing. Those who are stuck in one mode or topic may have the confidence to branch out and be more adventurous.

Just as with personal writing, the students need to have a commitment to the teacher-directed writing task if they are to be successful and learn anything from it. When you assign writing, you are taking some of the ownership of it away from the student. You will be making many of the decisions: what the writing is for, what form it will take, what the style will be. You can give the students a stake in the writing by doing some of the following:

- Create a need for the writing before assigning the task. For example, if you are taking the students to the zoo, they could list particular questions they would like answers to, write letters for information, make a planning chart for the day, and list ideas and words to use in a poem about their experiences.
- Never have students write for the sake of learning to write. Make sure there is a valid purpose for the writing (e.g., information to record, a letter to write, ideas to jot down so they are not forgotten), which the students understand.
- Make sure the students never write in a vacuum. Always provide a strong context for the writing. They need to respond to something, to create something, to record something. This might be a book they have read, an experience they have shared, or a project they are planning.
- Wherever possible, provide an audience for the finished product.

- Create situations in which the writing you want done is a necessary element. A science experiment can create a need for detailed observations and predictions. Notes may be taken during a group discussion so that they can be shared with another group.
- Provide opportunities for the students to share the writing they do. This could be through a bulletin-board display, in published books, in peer-group conferences, or in a story circle.
- Encourage collaboration.
- Use every writing opportunity to reinforce what you are teaching about writing as a drafting process.

When you are planning writing activities, you may find it useful to have beside you a list of possible modes and kinds of writing. Then you can record which ones you are having the students use. You may also want to keep individual records of kinds of writing each student has experienced and is comfortable with. Older students could probably do this for themselves.

Here is a list you could start with. Add to it when you see an opportunity for anything different:

Expressive Writing
- Exploratory writing, in which students formulate and think through a topic or question by writing about it
- Recording of experiences through personal narratives or letters
- Personal responses to literature
- Diaries
- Journals in which students write freely about thoughts and opinions on a variety of topics

Transactional Writing
- Organizing information
- Note-making
- Lists
- Charts
- Instructions
- Research reports
- Cumulative records
- Informational letters

Poetic Writing
- Imaginative narrative
- Using literary pattern
- Poetry

7
TEACHING THE SKILLS OF TRANSCRIPTION

Understanding Transcription

Transcription involves a number of different skills, such as: knowing letter shapes; printing and handwriting; punctuating; spelling; and practising neat, attractive presentation.

These tend to be the less interesting and more laborious aspects of writing. They are also the most noticeable, the ones that can create a good or bad impression before a reader even thinks about what the piece of writing is about. Therefore, whether we like it or not, they are very important.

As well as the technical aspects of transcription, we also need to teach the *concepts* of transcription: what it is for, why it is important, and when it matters.

What is transcription for, and why is it important?

Students will be more apt to spend time and trouble on transcription if they themselves see a real need for it. Here are a few things they need to understand:

- People will form an opinion of you based on how your writing looks, and how legible it is.
- If your writing is hard to read, often a reader – even a teacher – will give up and not bother to decipher all of it.
- Punctuation makes things easier to read and understand. Sometimes it can change the meaning of a sentence.
- Poor spelling can be disturbing for readers, and can make a stronger impression than your composition.

- Neatness and attractive presentation are a courtesy to your readers. They show you have taken trouble.

The best way for students to learn these basic truths is to offer them many different purposes and audiences for their writing. Transcription is more for the reader than for the writer. Therefore, without a reader it has no purpose.

When should it be done?

Children also need to know when transcription matters and when it does not. Few of us bother to recopy writing that no one is going to see. I don't care how messy my shopping list is; however, if I am making a list for someone else, I take a lot more trouble over neatness, spelling, and accuracy. We want children to put time and effort into transcription when it is called for – i.e., in a final draft – but we do not want them wasting time on it when it is not appropriate.

You can teach the concepts of transcription by doing some of the following:

- Do not make a final draft the necessary completion of all writing tasks. All writing will not be seen by others.
- Never ask students to recopy neatly when there is to be no audience.
- Do not criticize or congratulate students about spelling except at final editing stage. Show that it does not matter until then.
- Do not criticize or congratulate students about handwriting until the final draft is done. Show them that only then does it matter.
- Provide enough opportunities for them to display or publish their writing, so that there is a legitimate reason for neatness and accuracy.
- Always expect neatness and correct spelling in a final draft.

Teaching Transcription

Skills are best learned at the moment they are needed. Teaching is relevant when it helps us do a job we are engaged in.

Therefore, many skills are best taught within the context of the children's own writing. The students are more likely to understand new techniques if they can be instantly applied to their own writing.

The writing itself will often indicate which skill is best taught at a particular moment. For example, a piece containing dialogue is useful for teaching quotation marks. Therefore, the best thing is to look at the students' writing when you come to the editing stage, and choose one or two things to demonstrate to them. Doing it at this stage means that the students can focus fully on the skill you are teaching, because composition and organization will already have been dealt with.

Instruction may be done individually, during a conference, in small groups, or sometimes with the whole class. Each mode of instruction has its place in your writing program. Here are some ways you might decide which is best:

Individual Instruction

- For a very young child who has not yet begun to attempt writing, you might print while he or she dictates. This models the act of writing, and demonstrates that writing preserves one's language and one's message.
- Help a child who is at an early stage of invented spelling to listen for and print the consonant sounds of words.
- Demonstrate letter shapes for a child who has not learned them yet.
- Provide spellings of a few words the child needs for a specific piece.
- Ask the child to point to and read aloud the dialogue while you put in the quotation marks. The student can then join in and continue the task.
- Talk about the "sentence", and demonstrate the use of periods.
- "Talk through" the writing as you make suggestions. For example: "You are starting a new topic here; this would be a good place to start a new paragraph."
"This is the name of a place. It needs a capital letter."

- Pick out one or two spelling patterns you could teach. For example: "This word ends in 'ght'. Do you know any other words that might end this way?"
- Ask your students to record the names and authors of books they read in their personal reading time. Establish the practice that this should be done as neatly as possible, because it is to be a permanent record. This provides daily practice for young children in neat printing and letter formation, while keeping it in the context of a purposeful activity.

Small Group Instruction

- Bring together a group of students who are using dialogue and teach them how to use quotation marks. While they are learning the skill as a group, they can apply it immediately in their own writing. Checking each other's work gives them another chance to learn.
- Put students into pairs with scissors and tape to help each other with paragraphing. They can actually cut up their writing into sections, put together things that belong together, sort the pieces into order, and tape them together. The negotiation and decision-making that go on promote learning of the concept of paragraphing.
- When a child is sharing a piece of writing during a group conference, suggestions you make about specific words, paragraphing, or spelling will be attended to by the other students.
- If one child needs help with spelling during a group conference, the other children might be involved in the learning. For example, ask, "What other words do you know that start with 'ch'?"

Whole Class Instruction

This should be confined to those concepts everyone needs. It should generally be short and focus on one topic only.

- For beginning spellers, draw their attention to initial consonants in a chart story or "Big Book". Get them to suggest other words that start with the same sound.

- Choose a word from a reading experience and use it as a model to teach a spelling concept or pattern. For example: " 'Jumped' sounds as if it ends in 't', but it doesn't. It is always 'ed'. Let's make a list of words we know with this ending."
- If all the students are going to write and mail a letter, print the school address on the board to show how a letter is headed.
- Talk about what you are doing when the students are watching you write on the board. "These are called 'periods'. They show when I am ending one sentence and starting another. Where do you think the next one should go?"

Children Who Transcribe Poorly

As we have seen, there is a great danger that students who are poor spellers or have little control over their handwriting will draw the conclusion that they are poor writers. These students often write very little because they know they will make a lot of mistakes. Writing less will not help them either in composing or in transcribing. You need to encourage them to write more, not less. Here are some ways you can help them gain the courage to write:

- These students know what their problems are. Place emphasis on what they do well, rather than on what they do poorly.
- Do everything necessary to make them really believe that you are interested in what they have to say, rather than in their spelling or neatness.
- Reassure them that just because they are poor spellers they are not necessarily poor writers. Prove you mean it by focusing totally on their composition, rather on their transcription.
- At editing and final-draft stages, do not overwhelm them with looking things up, correcting words, and recopying. These are the students who have difficulty in these areas; therefore, choose only one or two things at a time to focus on.

- If a lot of writing leads inevitably to a lot of correcting, poor transcribers will not do it. Therefore, provide all the secretarial help they need, whenever they ask for it. This may help to reduce their anxiety.
- Provide alternate ways for them to have their compositions preserved: they may tell their stories; they may illustrate their stories and have someone else transcribe their words; they may use a tape recorder and then transcribe their own words. (See following section.)
- Provide time and help outside their regular writing periods to help them work on their weaknesses.
- In extreme cases, do not mention transcription at all until the students feel free to write. Keep this up for as long as it takes.

Using the Tape Recorder for Transcribing

There may be children in your classroom who have good ideas but either cannot or will not write them down. There are several possible reasons for this: they may not yet have the necessary fluency in transcription; they may see themselves as poor spellers, and therefore as poor writers; they may be afraid of getting things wrong, and therefore unwilling to take risks. However, they should not miss the joy and satisfaction of authoring, which provides the chief motivation for writing anything.

The tape recorder can be useful for these students, by enabling you to separate the different processes and skills involved in the writing process, and allowing students to focus on them one at a time. Here is an example of how you might work with a reluctant writing student:

- Talk with the child to help choose a topic for the writing, and to get ideas flowing.
- Have the child draw a series of pictures to tell the story or present the information. At this point the student is focusing on composition, the telling of a story, or the collection of ideas or information.
- Then have the child dictate the "writing" for each picture

into a tape recorder. The child is now extending the composition by focusing on language to express ideas.

- Having already authored the piece, the child can then turn to the task of transcribing it. At first, you, another student, or an adult volunteer might help with this part of the process, but most children can be persuaded to attempt to transcribe their own words. The main focus at this point is on handwriting and spelling.
- In order to share the piece, you or the child can replay the tape and read along with it.

This method of writing can have many benefits:

- All the skills involved in the writing process are attended to, but *one at a time*. The writers can therefore give each one full attention at the appropriate time.
- You may find the writing getting longer and more detailed, as the students are free to compose without the restrictions of printing and spelling slowing them down. Children will invariably tell you more than they will write. Children who have usually written very little are often amazed by how much they can write. They can never again get away with telling you they cannot write much!
- Students may be encouraged to take risks and try out more ambitious compositions if they are not worried about such things as spelling. They need to know that at the transcription stages they will get all the help they need, even to the point where someone else does the transcribing for them at first.
- Students who do not have difficulty with transcription can still benefit by using this method from time to time. For all writers, it reinforces the concept of writing as a process involving different kinds of thinking at different times.

How Spelling Works

We usually think of English as a non-phonetic language, composed of totally illogical spellings and pronunciations. Because there are so many different ways to represent the sounds of the language, we may regard spelling as difficult and largely random. Spelling instruction has usually focused on having students memorize words.

Our spelling system is not, in fact, totally random. We do not have to rely totally on memory. A good speller is not a person who has successfully memorized the largest number of words, but rather someone who knows ways to figure out the logic and patterns of words.

There are several types of cues that help us when we have to spell a word:

1. Sound Cues

Many of the sounds in words correspond to letters or groups of letters. The sound-symbol relationships are often predictable, and follow known patterns. For example, initial consonant sounds are usually represented by exactly the letter we expect them to be. There are many rhyming patterns, such as sit, fit, wit; tree, free, knee; etc.

2. Function Cues

Many patterns are used repeatedly, and relate to how a word is used. For example, verb tense endings and plurals are fairly consistent.

3. Meaning Cues

Often the meaning of a word helps us with the spelling. For example, if you link 'sign' with 'signal' and signature, you may remember the silent 'g'.

Using these three kinds of information helps us to create words we need to spell. Learning to spell is not just a matter of memorizing words. We must keep the number of words our students have to memorize as low as possible.

If students understand how the spelling system works, then they can come to feel they have some control over it. Spelling will no longer be a maze they wander through blindly, but a series of problems they have strategies for solving.

Remember: none of us learned all the words we can spell by memorization. Spelling is rather a skill of *constructing* words on the basis of patterns we know.

Developmental Spelling

The way children learn to spell is much like the way they learn to talk. They start by imitating what they see the people around them doing; then gradually, they come closer and closer to using standard forms.

When young children are learning to spell, they tend to show their learning in a particular and predictable sequence:

- They scribble in wavy, horizontal lines in an imitation of writing.
- They print a series of random letters.
- They print one consonant to represent each word. It is usually the first sound of the word.
- They begin to print a final letter as well as an initial letter. At this point they begin to put spaces between the words.
- Vowels start to appear in the middle of words. Often they are not the right vowels.
- All syllables and sounds in words are represented by letters.
- Finally, they make generalizations about spellings based on patterns they have noticed. Often they over-generalize. For example, when they have learned that a final "e" creates a long vowel sound, as in "bite", they will write "nite" and "frite".

At this point, children know enough about how spelling works to begin to build a repertoire of spelling patterns and add to their store of sight words.

It is this experience of constructing words on the basis of letter sounds and patterns that teaches children how spelling works. When they have reached a stage where they are close to standard spelling, they can begin to learn the many patterns and generalizations that enable us to be good spellers. Because there are so many patterns to learn, it will be years before young writers have enough experience and knowledge to be accurate in spelling. While they are learning, we must accept that there is much they have not had a chance to learn yet, and help them keep the faith that eventually they will become good spellers.

Teaching Spelling: Helping or Hindering?

How to Help the Learning of Spelling

- Publish and display children's writing, to create a need for standard spelling.
- Teach students that spelling is a thinking activity, not just a remembering activity.
- Teach students when, where, and why spelling matters.
- Encourage any attempt students make to spell.
- Help children to move to whatever the next stage of developmental spelling is for them.
- Provide information about words when students need it.
- Point out interesting facts about links between words, word origins, etc.
- Help children to link words into "word families" which have the same spelling pattern.
- Teach spelling by using groups of words that share a spelling pattern.
- Show the students how their knowledge about spelling is growing.
- Assess spelling proficiency in real writing contexts and at final-draft stage, rather than earlier.
- Encourage games and puzzles that involve words and spelling.
- Teach proofreading for specific things, such as plural endings.
- Teach students about the function of spelling patterns. For example, an "er" ending often indicates a person who does something (baker, teacher, etc.).
- Give regular instruction in spelling concepts, the patterns of words, and the construction of words.
- Inform parents about your spelling program, and help them to understand how their children are learning to spell.

How to Hinder the Learning of Spelling

- Expect to see accurate spelling at early stages in learning.
- Make spelling a major priority in your writing program.
- Teach children that all words have to be memorized.
- Expect students to look up all their errors in a dictionary.
- Require corrected spelling in every piece of writing the students do.
- Teach spelling by using lists of words that do not share a spelling pattern or generalization. (This makes memorization the only strategy for learning words.)
- Measure spelling proficiency by scores on tests.
- Draw conclusions about spelling ability by evaluating first-draft writing.
- Focus on children's weaknesses.
- Send home lists of words to be memorized.

Handwriting

The distinction between composing and transcribing is an important one. If children are practising printing or handwriting, they should not have the concerns of composing on their minds. Likewise, if they are deeply involved in composing, they should not feel they are practising handwriting at the same time.

Time and topic have as much to do with children's handwriting development as anything else. If children have enough writing time, and are comfortable with and in control of their topics, their handwriting tends to improve. When children have a well-chosen topic, their urge to express themselves dominates the writing time to the point that they lose track of the conscious aspects of handwriting and concentrate on the message. Thus, they become more relaxed in dealing with the mechanical aspects of handwriting, and as they write more and more, their handwriting improves.

You will need to provide many opportunities for students to focus on and practise their handwriting. Like all other learning, this will be most effective if it has real purpose for the students. Here are some examples of real-purpose handwriting practice:

- Writing final drafts that are to be seen by others provides the purpose and motivation for good penmanship. This final recopying is the time for the student to pay full attention to the handwriting without having to think about what to say, which words to use, or how to spell them.

- Let the students take over all the letter-writing in the classroom. If a letter needs to go home to parents, a student can write it. If a message has to be sent to another classroom, a student can write it.
- Teach the students how to keep their own records. This should always be done as neatly as possible. They can record books they have read, topics they have written about, activities they have completed. Even very young children can do this, if they know where to find the words to copy. Copying can always be handwriting practice, because there is nothing else the writer has to focus on.
- Have a bulletin board for students to use for their own messages. They can advertise things to swap, put up posters about upcoming events, record recess sports scores, or anything else that interests them.
- If you need a poem copied onto chart paper, or a chart story recopied in second draft, ask for a student volunteer. Don't always choose the one with the best handwriting.
- Become skilled yourself in calligraphy. Let the students see you taking pride in beautiful penmanship for special occasions. From time to time, print something they have written – a class book, or a collaborative poem – or a piece of your own writing in your own beautiful printing. Teach any student who is interested.
- Never write anything if you can ask a student to do it. Real purpose is what drives learning.

Process and Product

We are placing a lot of emphasis now on teaching the process of writing. In the old days the focus always seemed to be on the product. Some people believe that we make a choice about whether to be a process teacher or a product teacher. How do we reconcile these two aspects of writing in our teaching?

Emphasizing process has somehow come to suggest that spelling and neatness are no longer important. This is a misconception. Spelling is part of the writing process; if we are teaching the process, then we are teaching spelling. What process teaching really means is that spelling is not a focus all the time. The concept of process is correctly used when composing and transcribing each receive the focus due them at the most appropriate time. This is what we must teach our students about the process. It is not an either-or situation.

Process is *how* you do the task; product is what you finish up with. Without a knowledge of how to go about the job of writing there is no way to produce any satisfactory product. It is important for us as teachers to understand the processes involved; it is even more important for our students to understand. This is why the process must be an important part of our teaching.

As we have seen, when a writer sets out to do a piece of writing, he or she has some outcome in mind. The writing has purpose and possibly an intended audience. As the writing progresses, the writer gets an increasingly clear idea of what the finished product will be like. It is this product that the writer will be working towards during the successive drafts of the writing. The reader will also have certain expectations of the product. The writing will be considered successful if it fulfills both the writer's and the reader's expectations.

As a teacher of writing, I want to help a student achieve the desired product. In order to do this, I have to guide the student through the different steps of the writing process, working on a different aspect of the product at each stage. While the student focuses on working towards the product, my focus will be on teaching the student to use the process to achieve it.

Most of the pieces of writing that students create in my classroom are probably not of lasting importance. In a few years, or maybe even tomorrow, they will likely be forgotten. Therefore, the individual pieces of writing are not my primary concern. What I want from these writing experiences is some lasting learning that will enable my students to function as writers in the future. Each writing experience should teach something that can be used next time.

My ultimate goal is that the students be able to think and operate as writers. The more they understand the process of writing, and how it can work for them, the better their future products will be. Therefore, process will always be my focus.

In short, the process *is* my product.

8
EVALUATION

Evaluation as a Part of Learning

I remember the first mark I got in high school. As I arrived in science class, Miss Sawyer was handing back the first homework assignment. She called names and handed out papers, and threw in suitable comments as she went, so that everyone in the class knew what mark you had, and what stupid errors you had committed. When she got to mine, she said, " 'C'. That wasn't very good, was it?" I had no idea what she meant. In my little three-room primary school we had always been given marks out of ten. At least I figured out that "C" meant she wasn't very impressed. I found out in time that she docked marks if you didn't use a 2H pencil for diagrams. That was the same Miss Sawyer who, a couple of years later at a parent interview, told my mother I was "pretty mediocre". I give my mother a lot of credit for bursting out laughing.

This evaluation was useless to me; it did not help me do any better next time.

Then there was Miss Francis, my Latin teacher. In four years of trying, I never discovered the secret of Latin translation, let alone the purpose of it, even though, to Miss Francis, it was clearly filled with supreme joy and fascination. I was amazed when, on one report, she wrote that my syntax was improving. I had been teaching for ten years before I found out what syntax was. It wasn't often I was told I was improving in Latin. It was hard to repeat the experience when I didn't know what I had done right.

Again, the evaluation did not serve any useful purpose. Being congratulated on how well you did can be as non-productive as being told you failed.

Another highlight of my evaluation memories was the time a friend and I did our French homework together when she stayed at my house for the weekend. Susan was an A+ student in every subject. She finished up winning a handful of scholarships to Cambridge, and achieved such high marks that the Board of Governors gave the whole school an ice-cream and a half-day holiday to celebrate. After this weekend, Susan and I handed in word-for-word identical translations. She got an A, I got a B+. And my handwriting was as good as hers, if not better. Our teacher obviously saw Susan as an A and me as a B+. Inevitably, so did I.

This kind of evaluation was too general; it gave neither me nor the teachers useful information. How did it enable them to know how each of us needed to be helped?

I remember only one comment my English teacher ever wrote on my writing. Not only do I remember the comment, I remember exactly what I had written that she liked so much. We had to write a composition, no kidding, about what we had done on our summer vacations. I wrote about a day my family had spent in the New Forest. I used the phrase, "Out came bats and balls." She wrote in the margin, "nice". I thought it was nice, too. I got B+. This evaluation taught me something about how a reader responds to certain techniques in writing; it was information I could use another time to make my writing better.

Looking back as a teacher on my own schooling, I know that the education I received was a fine one. I wonder, though, how the evaluation practices contributed to the learning process. Every piece of work I did was solely for the purpose of evaluation. There was never a chance to experiment, to try something new. The only feedback came from the teacher, and that was always well after the fact. There was no other audience, no other purpose. When the evaluation was done, it rarely told me specifically what I had done well, what I should do to become better. Anyway, by the time I received the evaluation the piece of work was history; there was little point in working on it any more. I was judged, not helped.

The evaluation practices I experienced seem now to have been working against what my teachers wanted me to learn.

Whenever we assign a task that the student knows is going to be evaluated, we are setting up a test situation, not a learning experience. As a rule, we don't learn much by taking tests. Learning involves risk-taking, being unsuccessful a lot of the time, having a lot of practice before you get things right, gradually getting closer and closer to where you want to be. Motivation to learn involves feeling a measure of success, being aware of making progress, even when you are a long way from getting things right.

For evaluation to be of any use to the learner, it must come as an integral part of any learning experience. You need to know how you are doing while you are doing it, not later. Then you have a chance to figure out how to do it better. When I am learning something new, what I need is someone to understand what I am trying to do, and help me do it better – then get out of the way while I practise on my own. I don't need a critic, I need a coach.

We cannot learn anything unless we ourselves can judge how we are doing. I judge my progress as a pianist by noting whether what I play sounds right to me, and if it sounds any better than it did the last time I played it. If I need someone to tell me every time I make a mistake, then I may as well give up. I certainly don't need my errors totalled up into a score – or my successes either, for that matter. My piano teacher never felt the need to listen to me and judge me every time I played. I had every chance to practise before I was accountable. When I wasn't successful, she set me on the right road, and sent me away to practise some more.

It might be productive for us, as teachers, to help our students see ongoing evaluation as part of the process of doing a task, its purpose being to help each student be successful in the task. This is likely to support learning and be more productive than having evaluation seen as an after-the-fact assessment of how well the students did. It will also tell us far more about the students' learning processes, as we observe them at work.

Are students going to say, "Why should I bother to work hard, if I am not going to get a mark?" I have heard some people express this fear. This reduces teaching to the level of animal training, where you dish out a dead fish for every trick your seal performs. If students are only working for marks and teacher approval, our system is in serious trouble. What will happen out of school? If there are no intrinsic rewards in learning, then we will seek to learn nothing. If reading and writing have no purposes other than B+, then we have no motivation for literacy.

Assessment can be a help or a hindrance to learning. We have control over which it is to be. Evaluation must do more than support our teaching. It must be indistinguishable from it.

Developmental Learning

All learning is developmental. Whenever we set out to learn something new, we are probably not going to become instant experts. It takes a lot of will, a lot of practice, and the right kind of help for us to improve.

Children themselves have taught us about developmental learning, and all parents understand the concept. When children learn to speak, they start by imitating sounds they hear around them, some of them language, some of them not, often making noises just for the joy of hearing them. Then they learn to discriminate between sounds that convey meaning and those that do not. From this point on their babbling gradually comes to sound like language.

This growth from nonsensical babbling to meaningful language is a process that takes several years. The child coming into school still has many more years of experience ahead in which to become a more fluent and proficient user of spoken language. In fact, all our lives we are constantly refining, changing, and extending our range of talk.

This slow process of gradually moving closer to the goal we wish to reach is called developmental learning. It is a process of successive approximations, each one getting us a little closer to where we want to be.

The most natural way for children to learn anything is by this same process of successive approximations. This should affect our evaluation practices:

- If we want learning to take place in our classrooms, we must provide the right experiences, models, and help. Therefore, we should evaluate our own classroom

programs to make sure we are providing what each student needs.
- It is pointless and non-productive to look for accuracy in the early stages of any learning.
- We should not just be looking to see whether children have something right or wrong; this is not, by itself, useful information.
- We should not necessarily teach the correct way to do things. This might be too large a step for a student in the early stages of learning. Sometimes the best thing is to move a child forward one step at a time.
- We must be aware of developmental stages, so that we can guide our students through them. We have seen how students learn to spell by building up their knowledge in small steps, each one coming closer to standard spelling. If we know what the next step in learning is likely to be we can help our students take that step.

Tracing growth through developmental stages is one phase of an evaluation program.

When to Evaluate

We want evaluation to reinforce what we are teaching the children about how writing works. What we focus on, talk about, ask questions about, and respond to, will teach our students what we value. This is why the when of evaluation is as important as the what.

Suppose, for example, you are talking to a student about a piece of writing at a first-draft stage. What is it you hope the student will understand about first-draft writing? As I have noted you want the student to focus on content – ideas and language. Therefore this, and only this, is what you must talk about and respond to. If you as much as mention spelling or handwriting – even to congratulate the student on it – you are showing that this is something one should think about during first-draft writing. This is a false message about how writing is done. Similarly, if a student has been working to organize information, then organization is what you should respond to and evaluate.

What you need to do is to decide what, for the student, is the focus of the task at hand. This is what you want the student to concentrate on and learn about. Therefore, this is what *you* should concentrate on, both in teaching and in evaluating. One focus at a time is usually enough for an apprentice writer.

Here is a good rule to follow:

You are entitled to evaluate *only* what was the focus of the task at hand.

If you follow this rule, you will achieve the following:

- You will be teaching the student what is important at each stage in the writing process.
- You will be helping the student to work on one thing at a time. This always produces better results.
- The evaluation will be fair, because it exactly matches the task and the teaching.
- Because the evaluation is specific, it can be more useful in helping the student understand the task and know where the writing is successful and where it is not.
- Because the evaluation is specific to the task, it will enable you to keep more detailed records of the student's progress and achievements.

What to Evaluate

You might think of your evaluation in terms of three groups of skills:

1. Knowledge of the Writing Process

How to go about the task of writing

2. Composition

Skill in creating and organizing ideas and language

3. Transcription

Skill in recording compositions in standard forms of spelling and handwriting

1. Knowledge of the Writing Process

What does a writer need to know about the writing process in order to be successful? Here is a list you could start with:

- There are many different kinds of writing.
- Writing is not expected to come out right the first time.
- Writing is a drafting process.
- During first draft the focus is always on content. Form and transcription are not important at this point.
- Revision is intended to make the writing better – clearer, more interesting, more accurate, more organized.
- Good, standard English and spelling are important in a final draft.
- Writing that is to go public should be as complete, accurate, and attractive as possible.
- Some writing is just for the writer, and will not be revised, edited, or shared.
- Some writing is experimental and will not be finished.
- Not all writing is good enough, suitable enough, polished enough, to be seen by an audience.

If a student has misconceptions about any of these facts, the student does not understand the process. As you observe students at work and talk to them about their writing, you will build up a picture of their perceptions of the task of writing.

2. Composition

What are the elements of composition you want to look at in a student's writing?

When you prepare to look at a piece of writing, you need to know what it is you are looking for. You could make yourself a list of features that might be evident. Then, as you read, you can check off or note which of the features the student is using well, and which are not being used well. This will tell you what the student is able to do, and what you might help the student to develop.

The items on the list will vary according to the kind of writing the student is doing. If the work is an imaginative narrative, you might look for some of the following:

- What is your overall impression? Is it interesting?
- Is the story well organized? Do things flow along in a sensible order, without gaps? Are events linked together?
- Are the characters presented so that you know them, understand them, identify with them?
- Does the writer describe things well?
- Are the style and language suitable for the intended audiencc?

If the work is a research report, you might look for features like these:

- What is your overall impression? Is it interesting?
- Has the topic been covered in enough detail? Does the writer sound knowledgeable about the topic?
- Is the information organized sensibly?
- Is it just a repetition of facts, or are the writer's interest and opinions evident?
- How productively have research sources been used?

3. Transcription

When you look at a transcription, you should do so in light of the student's knowledge and experience:

- Is the handwriting neat and legible? Has the student taken trouble with the final draft? Is there anything the student needs special help with?
- Does the spelling represent the best the student is capable of at this stage? What does it indicate about the stage of spelling development? Is there a pattern in the kinds of errors the student is making? What could you teach through this piece of writing?
- How has punctuation been used? What does it indicate about what the student knows already? Is there anything that could be taught with this piece of writing?

If you start out with a basic list of the kinds of things you might see, you will find you add to the list other features you notice in the writing. Then, when you come to talk with the student, you will have specific things to comment on. You will know what has been done effectively, what is not working so well, and what you could teach the student at this time.

When you come to keep a record of a student's abilities in writing, you will have specific categories to consider. Your records can be quite precise and detailed. As you add to these records, you will see where growth is occurring and where it is not.

Asking the Right Questions

In the old days of marking, correcting, and grading, we used to ask one main evaluation question:

Is it right or wrong?

This is the "game show" system. There are no degrees of success; no indication of how close you are to being right; no help other than being shown your errors and supplied with "right answers". If you get enough right answers, you win the prize. Otherwise, you get nothing.

Now that we understand learning as a process, we can ask a more productive question:

Is the student getting closer?

This is the developmental system. It reflects what we know about how people learn. As we have seen, all learning is a series of successive approximations. As teachers, we have an ultimate goal in mind, a level of competence we hope our students will achieve as a result of their experiences and instruction, an end product towards which students are working over a long period of time. We need to know whether or not our students are moving closer to that goal. We would expect, for example, that their uses of language will become more complex, that their vocabularies will become more extensive, that their spelling will come closer to the standard. Asking the right question will enable us to note when students are making progress and advancing their learning, even when their language is still immature and their spelling far from standard accuracy.

Once we have asked the right question, and have information about how much a student knows, we need to figure out how to help the student take the next step. This involves diagnosis. When we see students making errors or using

104

language that is not standard, we must ask the second important evaluation question:

Why is it wrong?

Children do not use language randomly. There is always a reason for what they say or write. Understanding *why* they use a particular form can give us insights into what they know about language.

For example, four-year-olds typically start saying things like "wented" and "goed". If we ask the old question, "Is it right or wrong?" we come up with the information that it is wrong. If we ask, "Why is it wrong?" we discover that four-year-olds have learned the rule for making past-tense verbs and are trying to apply that knowledge in new situations. This kind of information completely changes how we view children's language learning, and what action we may take. In this case, no action is called for. Rather, we should expect more experiences with language to lead children to make a new generalization which includes exceptions to the rule.

Sometimes an error is made because a child has a misconception. For example, misspelling is often a result of mispronunciation, and this is something we can help the child correct.

Observing the Children

I can remember working away at my desk in school while the teacher patroled the aisles, looking over our shoulders. When the teacher stopped at my desk, everything I was doing seemed suddenly inadequate. I was afraid to do anything in case the teacher saw me make a mistake. I think we all developed hunchbacks, as we tried to shield our papers from the all-seeing eye. This kind of observation is not conducive to risk-taking.

Observation and assessment should not be made solely in order to troubleshoot. Especially in the beginning stages of a child's writing career, they should help both you and the child recognize progress and day-to-day victories.

There are two kinds of observation you might make – "long-distance" observation of groups, and close-up observation of individuals.

Observing Groups

From time to time, take a few minutes and let your eye wander around the room as your students work. You might cast your eyes around the whole class, or select a particular group for focus. Here are some of the things you might notice and write down:

- How do the students use materials, such as paper and writing instruments?
- Are some students moving around the room? What are they doing? Is it always the same ones who are moving?
- Are resource materials, such as dictionaries, being used? How? Do students seem to know how to use these materials?
- Are some students helping others?
- Are any students working together? How do they handle this?
- Do some students take a long time to settle into their work? Is it always the same ones? What seem to be the reasons?
- How many are actually writing?
- Which students look at ease? Which look uncomfortable?
- How do students use their time? Which seem organized and involved?
- What questions might you ask certain children during your next conference with them?
- What are the traffic patterns? Do you need to store materials differently to cut down this traffic?

Observing Individuals

Choose one child to observe for five minutes while he or she is writing. You might at first try to observe each student in turn. As you get to know them better, you might target a few you need more information about, and observe them on a regular basis.

You might actually sit next to a child, or find a strategic spot from which you can observe unnoticed. Make sure that your observation does not make the child nervous or apprehensive.

Often just the fact that you are watching will make the student behave differently.

Here are some of the things you might look for:

- What is the student's attitude towards the writing? Is this consistent with the child's usual feelings about writing?
- Does the student seem at ease?
- How long does it take the student to get started?
- What, if any, avoidance tactics does the student use (sharpening pencils, fiddling with paper, visiting, etc.)?
- How does the student use the page?
- Does the student compose while writing, or is the piece pre-rehearsed in the mind?
- Does the student write continuously, or is it a stop-and-start process?
- When the student encounters a problem, how is it handled?
- What seems to come easily to the student? What seems difficult?
- What aspects of transcription are automatic for the student? What has to be figured out?
- How much spontaneous changing and revising goes on during the writing? Does the student freely cross out and change things?
- What is the student focusing on? Is this appropriate to the stage of the writing?

Afterwards, you might like to discuss your observations with the student. Ask questions about what the student did or did not do. This may give you information about how well the student understands the act of writing. It may also raise the student's awareness of his or her own behavior patterns.

Variation in Quality

You may find that the quality and quantity of some students' writing varies greatly from day to day or week to week. This is to be expected; in fact, it can be a good sign. The child whose writing is much the same from week to week may be a writer who is not being challenged, not trying new ideas and formats, who is sticking with what is safe and predictable, who is not a risk-taker.

Students – and adults – who write only infrequently do not experiment much; their writing tends to become repetitive and stultified. When the students are in a comfortable, supportive writing environment, where they write for prolonged periods every day, they will be more willing to try new subjects, voices, forms of organization, and language. The more risks they take, the more their writing will vary in quality.

Fluctuations in the quality of writing should generally be seen as a positive sign. They show that the students are reaching for new levels of achievement; are experimenting with new ways of expressing, explaining, and recording. Whenever we try anything new, the chances are we will not be completely successful the first time; some experiments work, others do not. All experiments teach us something, though – to continue with the same procedure and improve our technique, to try a new way of proceeding, or to seek help.

When the students try something that does not work for them, you must make sure they understand that this is normal, an element in the writing process common to all writers, whatever their age or proficiency:

- Be honest with them; when they are not successful, help them to recognize this, and understand the reasons why.
- Make sure that the failure of a piece of writing does not lead the student to feel a failure as a writer. Show that you value the idea and the attempt.
- Reward and praise a noble, failed attempt more than a routine and adequate success.
- Help students reflect on their writing; get them to tell you what they were trying to do, and their explanations for why it did not work. This kind of understanding leads to productive learning.
- Together, plan an alternative strategy for the student to try next time.
- Develop a feel for knowing when to encourage the student to try again, and when it is better to abandon the writing altogether.

- Share in the student's satisfaction when a problem is finally solved. This satisfaction is the true joy of writing.

Of course, sometimes students produce poor work because they are tired or bored. We all get bored now and then, and isolated lapses shouldn't worry you, but if a student who has previously shown expertise begins to make needless mistakes over a period of time, you should watch carefully for reasons. It could be anything from trouble at home to boredom with subjects you have assigned.

Evaluating Your Program

In order to plan a classroom program you have two things to consider:

1. The Content of Your Curriculum

Every subject, whether it is composition, beginning reading, or nuclear physics, has a content. This content is composed of all the things you need to know to be successful in that subject. It includes understanding, knowledge, skills, and techniques.

2. The Way People Learn

It doesn't matter how expert you are in your subject, or how well planned the content of your curriculum is; if you are not presenting the material in a way that makes it easy for your students to learn, then you are not going to be a successful teacher.

This means that to be successful teachers of writing, we first need to know all about the process and how it works, and what it is like to be a writer. We must be artisans, practitioners of our craft, who write regularly. Secondly, we must know about language development and how children learn, and what is likely to help them in refining and expanding their skills as writers. Then we can provide the right experiences and the right help at the right time.

It is a good idea to make yourself a checklist to help you both in planning and in evaluating your writing program. To start your checklist, you could use the table of contents of this book, and check from time to time how you are addressing the many aspects of being a teacher of writing.

One key to successful and productive evaluation is to make what you evaluate match what you are teaching. Remember:

If what you are teaching and what you are evaluating
are not exactly the same, then one of them is wrong.

9
RECORD-KEEPING AND REPORTING

The Writing Portfolio

When an artist goes to apply for a job, he or she takes along a portfolio of work. This is a collection of representative samples which show the best work the artist can do.

In the professional world, writers are judged in the same way. We do not know how much Hemingway put in the garbage; his ability as a writer is assessed by looking not at his average, but at his best work. If a writer is truly trying to extend experience, to try new subjects and styles, to practise and hone his or her craft, then many false starts will be made.

We must assess our students as writers by these same criteria. If we build up a portfolio of each student's work, then we will have a permanent record of level of achievement, as well as growth and development.

Here are some suggestions for building up a portfolio:

- Periodically, perhaps at the end of each month, choose a piece of each child's writing to keep.
- Discuss with the student the pieces of writing in the folder. Ask the student's opinion about which is the best piece. Comparing pieces is a good way for the student to learn what makes one piece of writing better than another. It also tells you how the child feels about his or her own writing, and whether or not the child can step outside it and assess its worth from an audience's point of view.
- Tell the student which piece you think is the best, and explain why. This is one way of telling the student what he or she is good at, and where the writing has weaknesses.

- Negotiate which piece to keep in the portfolio. The sample might be chosen as typical of the child's writing at that time. It could be the child's best piece. It could be one that shows new learning – such as the first time a child uses spaces between words, or paragraphs.
- Date the sample you have chosen, and store it in a file-folder.

You can use these samples in a number of ways:

To show the student's progress to parents during interviews

This is particularly useful when you want to explain to parents why accuracy is not necessarily what you are looking for all the time. When you are talking to the parents, you can:

- point out areas of growth;
- highlight strengths;
- show evidence of risk-taking or non risk-taking;
- show areas of weakness you are working on;
- indicate where you are looking for growth in the near future;
- show parents how they can help at home.

To evaluate composition

- Use your lists of features of different modes of writing to do a detailed analysis of one or more pieces of writing.
- Compare pieces written at different times during the year to identify areas of growth.
- Write a summary of the student's ability for a report card.
- Update your own records from time to time.

To evaluate the student's use of language

- Look at the length, level of complexity, and sophistication in sentences and paragraphs.
- Note how the student uses language in different ways (for example, telling a story, giving directions, describing a scene, reporting, etc.).
- Note the student's use of language for reflection and thinking through ideas and concepts.
- Note the choice of words in poetic writing.
- Note the use of technical language in transactional writing.

To evaluate transcription
- Note the stage of developmental spelling.
- Note patterns in spelling errors.
- Note what punctuation the student is using well.
- Note legibility and style of handwriting.
- Note the student's ability to present work in an attractive form.

At the end of the year, or when the student leaves your classroom, choose two or three pieces to pass on to the next teacher, or to be stored in a central place as part of the student's ongoing evaluation record. In this way, your school can build up a picture of each student's growth over a number of years.

The writing portfolio will be your most complete and useful form of record-keeping. No other record, however detailed, will give as much information as having the child's actual samples of writing in front of you.

Anecdotal Records

You can look on anecdotal records as a kind of journal. You will be making entries in this journal whenever you note something new or different, or in any way significant about a student. These entries will be a summary and an explanation of the information you are gleaning from your observations of the student at work, and your analysis of the writing the student produces. You might include observations like these:

- Things you notice while you are observing the student at work
- Particular problems the student encounters, and how they are solved
- Changes in the kind or quality of writing
- How out-of-school factors are affecting the student in school
- Comments other teachers make about the student at work in other classes
- Your interaction with the student's parents
- A record of what is discussed in a writing conference
- Notes on a student's use of another language
- Notes about how a student operates – how topics are

chosen, how research is tackled, how revising and editing are done

Thinking of anecdotal records as your journal, rather than as a time-consuming record-keeping system, may help you develop a routine that lets you keep up to date without getting bogged down in paperwork. If your students write a journal every day, this might be a good time for you to write yours.

Here are some hints to get you started:
- Set up a binder with a page for each student. Add more pages as you need them.
- Have the binder nearby at all times.
- Have the binder at your side during writing conferences. After the student has left you, it doesn't take more than a minute to jot down any significant points you want to remember.
- When you target a group for "long-distance" observation, record what you notice in your journal.
- When you have observed an individual student, record what you see and how you interpret your observations.
- Date all your entries.
- File notes from parents, or any other relevant documents, right in the binder.
- Write the diary for yourself, not for an audience. Abbreviate, use shorthand, don't bother with complete sentences. Do anything you can to make it fast. It will likely not be published! You can always translate if you need to pass the information along.
- Every couple of weeks or so, browse through the journal and see which students you have written nothing for. There may be children you have missed, and you may want to pay special attention to them.

Checklists

Checklists are useful any time you have a list of specific things you are looking for.

You may be looking for them in a particular piece of writing. For example:

- Features of a story
- Facts to be included in a report
- Punctuation marks a student can use and proofread for

You may be looking for them over a long period of time. For example:

- Stages of spelling development
- Stages of reading development
- Kinds of writing a student has tried
- A student's understanding of the writing process

Checklists have many advantages:

- They do not take a lot of time to fill in.
- They can help you group students. It is easy to see, for example, which students are in the same stage of spelling development.
- You can see patterns emerge as checkmarks cluster in certain areas.
- If you use a date, rather than a checkmark, you can see rate of growth at a glance.

The best checklist is the one you make yourself:

- It will help you to clarify your own thoughts about what you think is important.
- It will give you a focus when you observe a student or read a piece of writing.
- You will be able to evaluate for specific points or features, and keep records of your findings.
- You will be able to make your checklists exactly match what you are teaching and what your students need to learn.
- Information you collect on your checklists may help you write your anecdotal journal, and put information at your fingertips when you are talking to the student, writing report cards, or talking with parents.
- A staff can develop checklists which can continue with each student throughout the school.

How To Make Your Own Checklists

1. An Observation Checklist

This is a checklist you might use while you are observing the students at work. To create this kind of checklist, make yourself a list of a few specific things you are going to look for. Use a class list, or a list of the particular students you are going to assess. Put your specific items across the top of the page. Leave enough space to add other points as you come across them in your assessment.

For example:

- Some students are not getting much down on paper during their writing sessions. You want to find out what it is they are doing. Your list might start out with your ideas about what they might be doing:

  - Collecting materials
  - Talking with friends
  - Sitting thinking
  - Writing, then crossing out
  - Looking up spellings
  - Sharpening pencils

    As you observe the students, you may notice other behaviors, which you can then add to your checklist. Over two or three observation sessions, you will be able to build up a checklist of possible behaviors you can look for when you observe students who are not getting much writing done.

- You have been helping some students focus on organization when they write research reports. You want to know what they are and are not able to do.

    Again, start out by making a list of features you think should be present in a well-organized piece of transactional writing:

  - Language is clear.
  - Facts are presented in a logical order.
  - It is clear what is fact, and what is opinion.
  - Lists, charts, and graphs are used where appropriate.

    As you read through some reports, add to your list

anything you think shows good organization. After a while, you will have built up a checklist you can use as a guide whenever you are reading research reports.

2. A Checklist for Growth over Time

This is a checklist you may return to from time to time throughout the year, or even over a number of years, to see what progress the student has made.

To make this kind of checklist, make your list of skills in the sequence you expect them to be learned in, from simple to more complex. At suitable intervals in the year, when you check the student's work, check off any new skills the student seems to be comfortable with.

For example:
- You want to trace growth through the stages of developmental spelling. List the steps you expect to see:
- Pseudo-letters in rows
- Random letters to represent sounds
- Initial consonants to represent whole words
- Initial and final consonants to represent words
- Etc.

Use a class list, or a list of the particular students you are checking. Write the skills you want to evaluate across the top of the page.

Update your checklist at regular intervals, perhaps at the end of each month, or whenever you notice a student showing characteristics of a new stage.

Children's development does not conveniently follow the ten-month calendar of a school year. Developmental checklists need to continue with them from year to year, and from teacher to teacher. It is a good idea, therefore, for you to get together with the other staff members in your school to develop checklists that can record growth throughout the children's school careers.

These checklists can form part of each student's evaluation profile.

The Evaluation Profile

Most elementary school teachers see students for only ten months. We spend the first month getting to know them and what they can do. Two months after that we are expected to write report cards as if we were experts on each child's growth and development. In another six or seven months we are getting ready to pass them on to another teacher.

In the days when we had a grade level standard against which we measured the children, and prescribed texts to tell us what they should know, perhaps this was satisfactory. It will not do today.

We know now that learning tends to happen in growth spurts and plateaux. We also recognize that the more we know about the students we teach, the better we can help them in their growth. We want the education of our children to be a continuous process of growth, not a series of yearly chunks. It makes sense, then, to see evaluation as a continuous process of building up a picture of what a student can do.

What we need is a way of recording and passing on information with the child throughout the school experience. One way to do this is by starting an evaluation profile. Set up a file for each student on the day he or she enters the school. Decide as a staff what kinds of information you will put into the file.

For example:

- Interest profiles
- Writing samples from the beginning, middle and end of each year
- Copies of anecdotal reports
- Developmental checklists
- Report cards

The file can also include information about the child's reading, other subjects, physical development, and anything else that gives relevant information about the child's functioning in school.

Wouldn't it be nice, when students leave elementary school, to have a complete record of their growth over five, six, or seven years? Both the students and their parents would be interested in looking back over writing samples and other accomplishments.

Reporting to Parents

During the school year, students receive many responses to their writing in draft and final forms. Consequently, ongoing evaluation and help are part of their writing activity from the beginning.

When you report to parents, to students, or to anyone else, they need to have the same kind of information you have been collecting regularly during the year. You need to answer several basic questions about each student, bearing in mind what it is parents really want to know:

- Is the student a motivated and hard-working learner?
- How competent is the student in handling the day-to-day work of the classroom?
- Is the student making satisfactory progress?

These three areas should be addressed in the report card you send home. They could also provide a focus for your discussions with parents in interviews, and with students from time to time in conferences.

Your records will put this information at your fingertips. You will have been monitoring these same three areas:

- The student's understanding of the purpose, process, and methods of working
- The student's strengths and weaknesses
- The student's growth and development

Writing a report card is largely a matter of picking out the most important points you want to deal with, summarizing your records, and using a language your audience will understand. People in the "business" of education – principals and other teachers – may be able to understand our checklists and notes; parents need these translated into lay terms which mean something to them.

Here are some other ways you can keep parents informed throughout the year about a child's progress and performance:

- Give parents concrete evidence of learning. For example, send home a copy of a recent piece of writing, along with an older piece from the student's portfolio. Attach a note on which you or the student list areas of growth you have seen.

- When a student makes a breakthrough in learning, send home a note celebrating the achievement.

For example:

Maria has just had her first book published this year. She worked hard to revise and edit her work to get it ready for publication. We would like to show you how she turned a rough first draft into a finished piece of writing. If you can come in on Friday at 3:00 p.m., please join the group while Maria shares her story with the class.

or:

Mahdu is bringing home a special story to show you. Because the story has a lot of dialogue, Mahdu has learned how to use quotation marks. He took total responsibility for this editing, and can use quotation marks accurately. The other students now know that he is an expert they can go to for help when they are editing their work.

- Make the parents welcome in your classroom. If they come to pick up their children, invite them in. Enlist their help as volunteers, either on a regular basis or for special events. Seeing how you and the students work will give them a better understanding of what you say about their children's writing.
- The students themselves are your best ambassadors. When students take their work home, make sure they know how to explain it to their parents. If they know what first-draft writing is, they can explain what the task was, what they have done so far, and what they have not yet done. If parents ask why work still has spelling mistakes in it, the students will be able to explain. If you use writer's language in the classroom, students will go home talking about drafting and editing.

═══ 10 ═══
THE LAST WORD

A School Writing Policy

Writing curricula are no longer based on a prescribed list of skills and rules or a set text, but on a system of beliefs and understandings about the subject, about how writers work, and about how children learn. Our classrooms have changed from places where we told children things to places where children experience and practise real life; from places where we made all the decisions in advance to places where we respond to children's special needs and interests, and share control.

It is more difficult, therefore, to explain what it is we do, not only to ourselves and to the students we teach, but also to parents. To make it easier for everyone to understand, it is a good idea to formulate for yourselves and your colleagues a school policy on the teaching of writing.

A school writing policy is a statement of beliefs about writing and the teaching of writing. It can have many benefits:

- In order to create a writing policy, teachers need to spend a lot of time talking through what they understand, and how they teach. This sharing of knowledge and experience is a learning experience for everyone concerned.
- If your policy is written down, it can be made available to new teachers, visitors to the school, and parents, to inform them about what you stand for, and why.
- It can help to present a consistent message to students about what writing is all about, and how they should do it. If a student is taught writing as a drafting process one year, and as a one-shot exercise the next year, we are working against ourselves.

Your language policy will be individual and special to your school, because it must be a consensus. It may change and grow over the years, as you modify it and refine it in the light of new knowledge and experience. In formulating your policy, you could start out by considering these three areas:

1. What We Believe about Writing

This will state your collective understanding of what writing is, and how writers work. It may include articles and recommended professional books.

2. How We Will Teach Writing

This may include experiences you want your students to have, ways you will organize your writing programs, and particular kinds of methodology you will use.

3. How We Will Assess Progress, Keep Records, and Report to Parents

This may involve devising checklists, setting up evaluation profiles, planning parents' information nights and newsletters, and designing a new report card.

Your writing policy will be, to begin with, a statement of intent about what you are aiming for. It can help you to make plans, to keep records, and to make meaning of your work with your students. Most important, it can make you, your colleagues on staff, your students, and their parents partners in the process of teaching writing.

Teaching and Learning

This book has no bibliography. This is not because it claims to be the only book you need to read about teaching writing, but because a list of such books would be too long. There are hundreds of books on the subject, and you really can't read too many. It is a good idea to build up a staffroom collection of professional books for your own use and reference, and for lending to interested parents.

Many books about teaching writing are by teachers sharing their own experiences and observations of their students. Why not set aside a lunch hour once a month for interested teachers to bring along writing samples from their classrooms? These could be great pieces of writing to be shared, problem pieces to be discussed, or pieces that show particular areas of growth. As we talk about writing together, we can gain deeper insights into what children are trying to do, how they show their learning, what their problems are, and what we can do to help. We can also find out how our colleagues respond to writing, and work towards some measure of consistency in the messages we are sending to students.

We cannot help any writer until we become skilled in looking at a piece of writing, noting its strengths and weaknesses, and isolating just what the writer needs help with at the moment. To learn this skill we have to read and respond to many pieces of writing. Like the children, we will not be very good at first, but can expect to improve with practice.

Above all, we must understand writing from the inside, as writers ourselves. Most of us have gained our experience of writing through school work and university essays. Recent experience is often confined to shopping lists, income tax forms, and the occasional personal letter. We need to do the same kinds of writing we are expecting and demanding from our students. Not until we think as writers can we begin to respond to students in an empathetic and helpful way. I know one group of teachers who meet at a pub after school from time to time to share their own writing.

It is very healthy, not to mention liberating, to be able to think of ourselves not necessarily as experts, but as professionals constantly improving our skills and learning from one another and from the students we teach. My hope for this book is that it will provide a starting point from which teachers can discover the real "basics" of teaching and learning about writing.

I belong to a generation for which writing for pleasure and personal satisfaction is extremely rare. I wonder if this needs to be so. My hope for our children is that they will become not only proficient writers, but enthusiastic writers; that writing will not only enable them to carry out the necessary tasks of life and work, but will bring them personal joy and satisfaction.